REDISCOVERING CHRISTIANITY

The True Gospel of Jesus Christ

By

Ravi Durairaj

Unless otherwise indicated, all Scripture quotations are taken from the *New King James Version* of the Bible.

Rediscovering Christianity

The True Gospel of Jesus Christ

ISBN-13:
978-1502306395

ISBN-10:
1502306395

Copyright © 2014 by Ravi Durairaj. All rights reserved

This book or parts thereof may not be reproduced in any form, stored in a retrieval system or transmitted in any form by any means – electronic, mechanical, photocopy, recording or otherwise – without prior written permission of the publisher, except as provided by United States of America copyright law.

Table of Contents

Table of Contents iii

Preface 1

Introduction 4

Chapter 1: The Primary Purpose of Creation 9
    Why did God Create Man? 10
    What is God Like? 11
    God Created You for Romance 13
    You Were Planned by God 14
    Love at First Thought 16
    You Can't Live Without Him 18
    Profound Intimacy 19
    Created Uniquely like God 21
    God has Given You All His Treasures 23

Chapter 2: The Incarnation 25
    Jesus Upholds All Things 26
    Jesus Was You 28
    The Ultimate Mediator 29
    Jesus Undid What Adam Did 30
    You are a New Creation, Just Like Jesus 32
    The Divine Reversal 32
    What Does This Mean for You? 34
    Did Father Forsake Jesus on the Cross? 34
    Purpose of Creation Revisited 37
    The Great Dance 38

Table of Contents

Chapter 3: God is Full of Grace 42
Grace Doesn't Mix with Works 42
God in Creation 43
Grace and Forgiveness 44
God Doesn't Think the Way We Do 45
Friend of Sinners 47
Is God Angry and Judgmental? 48
God's Judgment 49
Jesus Came to be Judged on Our Behalf 51

Chapter 4: Grace and Sin 53
Our Old Nature is Dead 54
The Grace Message and Sin 55
Living from Our Identity 57
God's Word Empowers Us 58
Holiness is Not Progressive 59
The Final State 60
The Consequences of Sin 61
You are Free from Sin 62
The Old Dual Nature Model of Living 63
Holy Spirit and Sin 63
You are Holy, Righteous and Perfect 64
You are Like God 66

Chapter 5: Grace, not Works 67
The Do-Get Paradigm 67
I Am vs. I Am Not 69
Salvation Isn't Just Spiritual 71
The Perfect Law of Liberty 72

Table of Contents

The Law was Never God's Plan for Us 74
Behold and Be Who You Are 75
Faith is by Grace. Faith is Not a Work 78
Christ in You, the Hope of Glory 78
The Finished Work of Christ 79
Was Jesus a Grace Teacher? 80
How Does God See You? 82
God is Better than Good 83
God Isn't Mad at You 84
No More Law 87
You Don't Have the Sin Nature 88
God Created us to Enjoy Life 89
No More Distance, No More Delay 91
God is Closer Than the Air You Breathe 91
Here and Now 92
True Freedom in Christ 92

Chapter 6: Are we only 1/3 Saved? 95

A Brief History of the Grace Movement 96
    The Patriarchs of the Protestant Church 96
    The Heroes of the Grace Movement 97
The Big Picture 98
Man is Resistant to Change 98
The Original Gospel 99
Is Man a Tri-Partite Being? 100
The Dualistic Mindset 101
My Salvation Experience 102
Struggle Between the Spirit and Flesh? 103
What is Sanctification? 105

Table of Contents

Chapter 7: The Inclusion Question 109
- *What is Inclusion?* 109
- *Are All Forgiven by God?* 109
- *Are All Reconciled to God?* 110
- *Is Everyone Saved?* 111
- *God's Side* 111
- *What Does Saved Mean?* 112
- *Holistic Salvation* 113
- *What is Faith?* 114
- *What is Union with God?* 114
- *How do We Live in Union with God?* 115
- *Grace and Inclusion* 115

Chapter 8: Living Under an Open Heaven 116
- *Introduction to an Open Heaven* 117
- *Jesus Obtained Access to an Open Heaven* 117
- *The Veil that Separated Us from God* 118
- *Did God Turn His Face from Mankind?* 119
- *Heaven has Invaded Earth* 120
- *In His Image* 121
- *You are a Living Open Heaven* 121
- *Keys to the Kingdom of Heaven* 123
- *You are a Royal Priesthood* 124

Chapter 9: The Kingdom of God 125
- *Ever-Increasing Kingdom* 125
- *New Testament Kingdom Revelation* 127
- *The Seven Spheres of Society* 128
- *Heaven is the Standard, Jesus is the Model* 129

Table of Contents

The Tree of Life *130*

You as God *132*

Kings and Priests *133*

Big God little devil *135*

Prayer Model *139*

Chapter 10: Effortless Living in His Amazing Grace **141**

Enter His Rest *142*

You were Designed to Live Effortlessly *144*

Grace isn't Laziness *146*

Healthy and Whole *147*

Who is the Wisest Person on Earth? *149*

How to Live in His Wisdom *150*

Hakuna Matata *152*

Forgiveness *154*

Judgment and Anger *154*

What is Your Destiny? *156*

Guilt, Shame, Insecurity and Fear *156*

Scenario 1: Before 1985 .... *156*

Scenario 2a *157*

Scenario 2b *158*

Trying to Become Who You Already Are *159*

The Grace Model *159*

Notes **162**

Chapter 1: The Primary Purpose of Creation *163*

Chapter 2: The Incarnation *163*

Chapter 3: God is Full of Grace *164*

Chapter 4: Grace and Sin *165*

Table of Contents

Chapter 5: Grace, not Works... 165

Chapter 6: Are we only 1/3 Saved? 167

Chapter 7: The Inclusion Question... 167

Chapter 8: Living Under an Open Heaven........................... 168

Chapter 9: The Kingdom of God 168

Chapter 10: Effortless Living in His Amazing Grace 168

Preface

The majority of the church has profiled God as a law-giving God who is angry when man disobeys Him. We have been influenced by our culture, our mythologies and by other religions and created a God who isn't much different from a pagan God. We have imagined that the primary aim of the Christian walk is to please a God who is waiting to reward the just and punish the unjust. We have created an elaborate religion based on these basic assumptions. Almost all translations of the bible reflect our understanding of God based on this model. We have built a whole belief system based on our theories of sin, guilt, repentance and forgiveness.

We have strayed further and further away from God's original intent of creation. We have placed God far away in heaven somewhere who cannot be reached. We have portrayed the main goal of the Christian walk to be one of a gradual lifelong process of purification that will hopefully take us to heaven some day. Till then, we feel that we live here on our own, praying to a distant God who is far removed from the day-to-day woes of humanity. We believe that the world is deteriorating and that God is withholding His pent-up fury from us. Many of us also believe that God is about to reach the limit of His patience and that He will soon release His wrath on us and destroy the world. We think that He will then reap the wheat and banish the chaff to eternal agony in hell.

Because of such a warped belief system, Christians spend their lives in fear and guilt, constantly trying to please an angry, judgmental God. Instead of living a life of freedom as God intended us to live, we live a life of bondage filled with guilt, insecurity, fear and shame. We think our life in this world is one of deprivation and wretched misery, and that some day all our dreams will be fulfilled in heaven.

We also believe that God will reward us based on how well we win others to such a belief system. We have created outreach programs to reach the lost and wonder why we are not experiencing good results. The people of the world don't seem impressed by our theories about God and don't see much incentive in believing in a God whose people live such a wretched, miserable life. They would rather enjoy their life without God than be trapped in a life of bondage like us.

Here is the general theory of the Christian belief system:

God created Adam and Eve in Eden and asked them not to eat of the tree of the knowledge of good and evil. Man disobeyed God and caused God to be infuriated. God banished man from His presence because He is holy. A holy God cannot associate with sinful man. God then came up with a system of laws. Man would be blessed if he kept the laws, or else he would be cursed. God then instituted a system of temporary sacrifices by which man could attempt to come into His presence.

God then sent His Son Jesus to be a sacrifice for humanity. Jesus came and bore the brunt of God's wrath on behalf of man to appease the anger of God. Now man can approach God on the basis of the sacrifice of Jesus. Now God can look upon man because of what Jesus did. Jesus came to live on earth and gave us an expanded set of laws. We can please God if we keep all His laws. If we are not diligent in obeying God, we will risk incurring His wrath and displeasure. We could lose our children or be inflicted with a disease. We could be punished and experience lack. Our failure to please God in every way could cause Him to bring auto accidents upon us. We could experience failures in our marriages and other relationships because of our disobedience. We think that as mere humans, we cannot live without sinning. So we ask his forgiveness when we sin and His blood cleanses us, so that we can get back into the good graces of God temporarily until we sin again.

Preface

We also think that this life is temporary and is just a journey to heaven. This life is filled with sin, sickness and hardships. When we die and go to heaven, all our woes will be past and our tears will be wiped away. While we are here on earth, we can get extra credit for reaching the lost and winning souls. We spend our life storing up treasures in heaven.

We present this as the gospel to people of other religions and to those who don't know God and wonder why we don't see results.

You may not believe exactly as I have described above, but most Christians have their belief system structured around something similar to this, with some slight variation, depending on their brand of Christianity.

We don't see positive results, so we come up with different methods of making our version of the gospel more attractive. We stir people up to perform signs, wonders and miracles, and then present our same works-based gospel to them, getting some results, but still wonder why we don't see a widespread adoption of our belief system.

Most of us have lived our lives accepting what others have taught us, without questioning the basis of our beliefs. I have always desired to understand the true meaning of life and our purpose for creation. Whenever the Lord led me into some truths, I always desired to know more. I sought the Lord for more and more and dug deeper and deeper into the realities of life. In this book, I would like to share what I have learned in the past few years with you. In the first few chapters, we will look at the true nature of God. We will look at the new covenant the way Paul preached it. We will then understand our true identity. We have always been trying to become someone better. God has created us in His image. We will see what it means to live out of who we are, someone who has been created uniquely in the image of God.

We will then look at the primary purpose of creation. This will revolutionize your life and help transform your understanding of your reason for existence. We will follow this with the meaning of the Incarnation. We will understand our important place in God's grand scheme of creation.

The last few chapters will reveal how powerful you are, equipped with the fullness of the power of God. Life may have been a struggle to you. You will begin to understand how to live a joyful life in union with God, in complete freedom, free from all bondage of sin, guilt, shame, unworthiness and insecurity.

Introduction

What if it turned out that our entire belief system was based on faulty assumptions and on a flawed foundation? What if God knew what He was doing when He created man? Perhaps God created the earth to be an extension of heaven and created the earth as an environment for man to experience heaven.

What if when man sinned, he didn't incur the wrath of God? Was it man who saw God in a different light and was filled with guilt and shame, which caused him to move further and further away from God?

Is it possible that God created man for the purpose of a close relationship with Himself here on earth? Could it be that God loves man in a way that far surpasses our understanding of love?

Could it be possible that God doesn't have any inclination of judgment in Him towards man and is not angry with man? What if God is angry, not at man himself, but at the sin that separates His beloved creation, man, from Him? I know this may sound preposterous to us, as most of us cannot imagine a God free of judgment and anger. This has become an integral part of our belief system, both culturally and through our studies and teachings.

Did God know before He created man that man would sin? Could God possibly have foreseen the fall of man and have already prepared a remedy to the fall? Could it be that God solved the problem of sin and has provided man with a means to live life fully, free from every form of bondage?

Is God a good God who just wants to bless us every step of the way? Just imagine that! What if all He wants to do is bless us and keep on blessing us no matter what we do. Could it be

Introduction

that His 'laws' or his 'enhanced set of laws' in the new covenant were just to provide us the guidelines to walk in His blessings and everything that He has provided for us freely? What if it is just our actions that are depriving us of some of His blessings and preventing us from walking in the fullness of all that He has provided for us? Is it possible that He has a Utopia for each one of us right here on earth?

Could it be that He had planned all along to come and live our entire lives here with us, as a part of us. What if He is right here with us even in the midst of our struggles, and has given us the abilities to live an abundant life filled with joy always?

Are we a part of His plan for the earth. Is it possible that you were handpicked for an extraordinary assignment and created uniquely to fulfill His master plan here on earth?

What if He created you to enjoy life on earth and be happy? Or taking it a step further is it possible that He wants to enjoy life on earth with you?

In this book, we will see God for who He really is, as a loving, gracious Father who has only our best interests at heart. We will look at how He created us in His image for the purpose of union with us. We will realize that God created us to be compatible with Him, and that we are His favorite form of existence. Our eyes will be opened to the fact that God enjoys living in unity with us in this world. We will see that Jesus came to earth because we are so precious and valuable to Him. He came to rescue us and deliver us so that we could live a life of freedom, filled with His love and joy. We will understand how He placed us on earth and has provided us with everything that we could possibly need for life and godliness. We will get an understanding of His divine plan to include us in the family of the Triune God who has been living a joyful abundant life from eternity. He has now included us in the fellowship of the Triune Godhead so that we can enjoy eternal, abundant life every moment of every day in this life. Once we realize that together with God, we can transform the world around us to bring heaven to everyone that we come in contact with, our life will be full of new meaning and purpose.

Introduction

We should be real people
Who live fully,
Love deeply,
Give totally
And enjoy life immensely

Chapter 1: The Primary Purpose of Creation

In this section, we will look at the primary purpose of creation. Understanding our beginnings and the purpose for our existence will give new meaning to life.

I watched the interview of a world-renowned singer recently. A few years ago, she was listed as the fourth-wealthiest performer in the entertainment industry—someone famed for her gifted singing and dancing abilities. At one point the interviewer said, "Now, let's look at what she's doing in her native country—Columbia." He went on to say that she had recently funded a state-of-the-art school in Columbia for about 2,000 children and had made plans to fund four more such schools, two of them in other countries. Then the interviewer asked how a glamorous singer like her had become a philanthropist. She said that there came a point in her life when she thought there had to be much more to life than just singing, shaking her hips and making money. In fact, she found new purpose when she realized her identity was far more than her talent to entertain people. This opened her eyes to see the desperate needs of the children in her homeland.

***

If you're like most people, there was a time when you were young and enthusiastic, anxious to make your mark on the world. You probably dreamed of meeting a wonderful mate you could love, someone who would love and marry you, so you could go on to live happily ever after. By now you may have married and perhaps even found your ideal career, only to discover that it's fallen far short of your dreams. Maybe your life feels like an endless roller coaster ride, but it's moving too fast to stop and let you off, and the whole scene has left you bored, disillusioned or even depressed.

If this describes you, I have great news for you. Believe it or not, you were actually born for a purpose—your destiny planned by a Grand Designer. And once you discover who you were meant to be and glean a glimpse of your purpose, I guarantee that you'll never be the same again.

Why did God Create Man?

First I'd like to ask the following question: Why did God create man?

Some believe that because God was bored He created man for His entertainment. This is the classic Greek god paradigm from which we get Greek mythology and classic films about Hercules and other mythical characters.

Others imagine an angry God who created mankind in order to avenge His fury. In this model He would send those who misbehaved to hell, and take the cooperative ones to heaven.

Still others have been taught that God created man to worship Him. That leads us to ask this question: Did God have self-esteem issues that required Him to create 7 billion people to worship Him in order to feel better about Himself?[1]

The truth is that God is completely self-sufficient and self-existent. He has absolutely no ego issues. The Creator doesn't need anyone or anything. While creation absolutely depends on the Creator for life, breath and sustenance, the Creator does not need the creation. He existed for eternity before creation. The Creator doesn't need creation, but creation needs the creator to exist.

Now, let's delve into why God created man.

Chapter 1: The Primary Purpose of Creation

What is God Like?

Deuteronomy 6:4 says, "Hear O Israel, the Lord our God, the Lord is one."

What does the Bible mean by the phrase: 'The Lord is one'? The Lord is one in that He is consistent with His nature. He isn't unpredictable or in conflict with Himself, angry one day, and loving the next. He isn't schizophrenic. God is love. His love never changes and never fails. His every emotion stems from His deep and abiding love and yearning to protect and preserve you and me. His qualities and characteristics are not in conflict. Even His anger is only to support His love. He has never been angry with you. The Greek word for anger is orgé, which means impulse, wrath. The word 'wrath' isn't a correct translation of orgé. This word is indicative of unrestrained passion. He is passionately angry at the sin that draws you away from Him; the sin that separates you, His beloved from Him. He feels nothing but gentle compassion for you and wants the best for you. In fact, He is doing everything He can to draw you, His beloved, into a close relationship with Him[1].

He is also one in that His personality is consistent within Himself: God the Father is in perfect agreement, that is, consistent with Jesus, the Son, and Jesus is in perfect agreement, consistent with the personality of the Holy Spirit. In other words, God doesn't have two opposing sides that required Jesus to come to earth to die in order to pacify His angry Father. Scripture says that Jesus came as the exact representation of God[7]. Colossians 1:15 says "The Son is the (exact) image of the invisible God" (Emphasis mine).

In fact, Jesus said in John 14:9: "If you have seen me, you have seen the Father."

Jesus also said: "I only do what I see the Father do. I

only say what I hear the Father say." 1 John 4:12 tells us "No one has seen God at any time."

That's exactly the reason Jesus came to show us what God was like. If you want to understand the nature of God, just look at Jesus.

Jesus was talking about the Holy Spirit in John 14:16 when He said this: "I will send you another Comforter." The word for another comforter is 'Allos Paracletos'. *Allos* means another of the same kind. When Jesus promised another comforter, He meant another just like Him. The Holy Spirit is just like Jesus.

God is also more than one in the fact that God is love[2]. It doesn't say God has love. God couldn't have existed for all eternity by Himself (singular) if He was love. If He had been by Himself (singular) for eternity, then love would have been something that He acquired along the way from outside Himself. Love simply can't exist by itself. Love needs an object to love.

In Genesis 1, we read, God said, "Let there be light." "Let the earth bring forth . . ." "Let the waters abound with living creatures" and so on. The word for God, 'Elohim', is actually a plural word. God is one being, but three entirely distinct persons: Father, Son and Holy Spirit. God existed in this relationship of love for eternity. Father, Son and Holy Spirit have been overflowing with extravagant love for each other and boundless joy, enjoying themselves since eternity. We can glean some insight into the relationship between the triune Godhead from what Jesus said in John 17:21-23: " . . .that they all may be one, as You, Father, are in Me, and I in You; that they also may be one in Us, that the world may believe that You sent Me. And the glory which You gave Me I have given them, that they may be one just as We are one: I in them, and You in Me; that they may be made perfect in one, and that the world may know that

You have sent Me, and have loved them as You have loved Me."

John 17:22 talks about the relationship between Father and the Son, and the oneness between them. Verse 21 reveals His purpose for humanity—that we be united as one, as the Son is one with Father. Verse 23 describes what motivates this desire: love.

His love and joy were so abundant that they overflowed into the expression of the act of creation. His amazing love flowed out of His abundant grace. The result was creation. This love overflowed into the creation of man because God wanted to share this love and joy that the triune God has been experiencing for eternity.[1]

God Created You for Romance

God created you for romance. This is the motivation behind all of creation—He included us in the romance of all romances—the romance of the ages. This is the purpose of creation. As I'm sure you know, rules and regulations shatter any semblance of romance and fun. Francois Du Toit tells us in Romans 7:6 (Mirror Bible)[2] "The moment you exchange spontaneity with rules, you've lost the edge of romance."

Rules and regulations were never God's ultimate plan for man. God created us for intimacy and oneness with Himself and our fellow human beings.

Ephesians 1:4 says "just as He chose us in Him before the foundation of the world, that we should be holy and without blame before Him in love."

Before the foundation of the world He planned for you to be included in the awesome fellowship of abounding love and overflowing joy that the triune God has been enjoying from eternity.[1]

Jeremiah 1:5 says "Before I formed you in the womb I knew you; before you were born I sanctified you."

On his website Mike Miller has a message series called 'Relax'[2] where he makes this statement: "Humanity was not adopted as sons at the cross. The cross was an event that became required because of the fall of man and redemption became a necessity. Adoption was predestined. The fall of man was foreknown, but not predestined. God knew that because of the fall of man, redemption would be a necessity. But the cross and redemption were not predestined. Galatians 4:5 says 'that we might receive the adoption of sons.' The adoption of sons wasn't given as a result of the cross. It became revealed to fallen man because of the cross. Adoption as sons was the original purpose from before the foundation of the world. Ephesians 1:4 says that from before the ages, we were chosen in Him. Man lost the revelation of his son-ship in the fall. In his own heart he became nothing more than a slave. He had to receive the revelation of that which was true from before the foundation of the world. Jesus didn't have to die in order for man to be adopted as sons. Jesus died because man had fallen and redemption became a secondary necessity."

Love needs only one thing—it needs to give. He wanted to include you into the divine family and give you everything He has—all His treasures. He included you into the divine fellowship because of His abundant grace out of His sheer goodness, just because He wanted to.

You Were Planned by God

In John 1 the Word says: "In the beginning was the Word, and the Word was with God, and the Word was God."

The Greek word for 'Word' is 'logos'. It encompasses both thought and speech. Christ is related to God in the same way that the Word is related to the idea. The Word includes the idea and the expression of that idea. Logos is Christ, the expression of the thoughts of the Father through the Spirit. Logos encompasses the thoughts and plans of God. It also includes God's design process and the expression of that design.

God didn't create everything out of nothing. The world was intricately designed and planned in the mind of God (as the Logos) from eternity. You were in the thoughts of God from eternity. God masterfully thought of you and intricately and uniquely designed you in His image. He dreamt about creating you from eternity for the purpose of love. You are His love-dream come true.[1]

This is very important for us to understand. You are not just one out of 7 billion people that just happened to appear out of nothing. God intentionally created you because He wanted you. And He decided He wanted you before you were conceived in your mother's womb, before you had any opportunity to please or disappoint Him.

Do we continue to love our children even when they're disobedient? Absolutely! Occasionally, we hear of parents disowning their children for extreme behavior, but God doesn't do that. If that is your view of God, it's probably reflected in your relationships, and I would recommend that you search out books on the Father heart of God. God hasn't changed His mind about you because of your behavior.

The Incarnation is proof that God hasn't changed His mind about you. Jesus came, not to choose some people and send others to hell. He came because He loved everyone in the world and He didn't want anyone to perish in sin. He came to give everyone who believes eternal life. Perhaps you noticed that I just paraphrased John 3:16. Obviously, we have a part to play in accepting His love.

1 Timothy 2:4 says: ". . . who desires all men to be saved and to come to the knowledge of the truth."

2 Peter 3:9 goes on to say: "The Lord is not slack concerning His promise, as some count slackness, but is longsuffering toward us, not willing that any should perish but that all should come to repentance."

We have been so exclusive in our views of God, that we only allow the few we think are worthy of His acceptance and exclude all the other vile, undeserving sinners, condemning them to hell. Thank God, He isn't intolerant as so many of us have made Him out to be.

Love at First Thought

Your existence, who you are, was established when God first thought of you.

Psalm 139:16 (ESV): "Your eyes saw my unformed substance."

You have heard of love at first sight. But when God thought of you, it was love at first thought. It is humanly impossible to love at first thought. Only God can love at first thought and He did! He created you to lavish His love upon you. This was His abounding grace in action. He thought of you and dreamt about you from before creation. You've been on His mind constantly since before creation and you still are. His desire is for you to be one with Him for eternity.

He loved you so much that He created the universe for you to live in. You love your children so much that you want to buy them the best clothes. You want to feed them the best quality food you can afford. You want to take them to the best places to eat. If you were a wealthy person, you would buy them the best quality car. You would give them the best education.

You wouldn't allow them to have anything inferior. Consider this: God's love for you is far greater than your love for your children. His love for you is an amazing, unconditional love, an incomparable love, a relentless love, a love that reaches higher than the highest mountain, deeper than the deepest sea. His love is an everlasting love, an unchanging love. He has been dreaming of you from before the foundation of the world.

When we begin to understand that we are not an accident and that we are of immense value to God, our perception of ourselves will change. This will help us with the self-image issues that may still be driving us to seek fulfillment in destructive habits.

The story of the ugly duckling is well known in the West, but hardly anyone in Eastern cultures, has heard of it. I love telling that story and seeing the lights go on in the minds of those who've never heard it. I love the part where the ugly duckling was deeply depressed because she was so unlike her brothers and sisters who mocked her and called her ugly because she looked different. One day she saw a beautiful swan in the distance and thought, "I wish I was beautiful like that swan." Nearly every day the wind whipped the water into choppy waves, until one calm day she was wallowing in her misery when she looked down at her reflection and saw a beautiful swan! She realized that she wasn't an ugly duckling, but a beautiful swan and stretched her majestic neck to its full length and gracefully swam toward the flock of swans in the distance, never again to associate with the ducklings.

In the same way, the moment you realize who you are: how precious you are to God; how flawless you are, you can instantly transform into your true identity. From that moment on you just need to be who you are. Song of Solomon 4:7 says, "You are all fair, my love, and there is no spot in you." You don't have to pray and fast to become who you already are. You would pray because you love God and want to spend time with Him.

You Can't Live Without Him

Let's look at another beautiful truth from Genesis Chapter 1.

In Genesis 1:11-12, God created trees, plants and grass from the earth. The literal translation would be "Earth, bring forth grass, trees, herbs . . ." The trees, plants and grass were created out of the earth, and can only live in the earth. They would die if removed from the earth.

In Genesis 1:20, 21, God created the fish and the sea creatures from the waters. The literal translation would be "Waters, bring forth living creatures, fish . . ." Fish and the sea creatures were created from the waters and can only live in the water. A fish cannot live outside water. Hence the term "Like a fish out of water."

In Genesis 1:26, God created man out of Himself. The literal translation would be "Us, bring forth . . ." Father, Son and Holy Spirit spoke and said "Us, bring forth man . . . in our image, in our likeness." God created man from Himself. Just as trees, plants and grass that were created out of the earth can't live without the earth, and just as fish and water creatures can't live out of water, man can't live without God.[1]

God designed man to live in closest proximity to Him. Man can live only if He lives in intimate fellowship and union with God. You may ask "How about those who are living out of fellowship with God?" Well, in reality they're not really living at all. When man doesn't live in fellowship with God, he isn't really living the full, abundant life that he was designed to live. He merely exists.

Chapter 1: The Primary Purpose of Creation

I love the song that we sing at our church. It goes something like this "I can't live without You! I can't breathe without You!" So true! You can't live without God! Every cell of your being was designed to be intricately interwoven with Him.

Profound Intimacy

Psalm 139:14-15 says: "I will praise You, for I am fearfully and wonderfully made; Marvelous are Your works, and that my soul knows very well. My frame was not hidden from You, when I was made in secret, and skillfully wrought in the lowest parts of the earth."

You are His intricate craftsmanship. You are His masterpiece. They say Michelangelo and his team of artists took several years to paint each of the breathtaking murals in the Sistine Chapel in Rome. My wife Selvi and I were awestruck when we saw Michelangelo's 'Pieta' in St. Peter's Cathedral in Rome. 'Pieta' is a sculpture of Mary holding Jesus in her arms after His crucifixion. If Michelangelo could create such splendid works of art, how much more perfectly do you think God has created you?

God designed you in eternity, perfect in every way. He dreamt about the wonderful creation that He designed for the primary purpose of intimacy with Him. You are fearfully and wonderfully made, for the pleasure of the King of the universe. You are the perfect product of His imagination and creative genius.

If you were God, you might have created a few hundred people to enjoy your love. You might have created a mansion for each one of them, surrounded by a beautiful garden, with fruit trees, vegetable patches, and maybe a few cows and some chickens and called it good.

But God's love has no limits—it is without height nor

length nor depth. He lived in this relationship of love—the love between Father, Son and Holy Spirit—a love that has existed for eternity—a love abounding with joy, honoring one another in perfect harmony. The love of this God, one being but three persons—simply could not be contained. Creation is the expression of the overflow of God's abundance in ways He had never expressed until He created us—the object of that love. His love was so abundant that it overflowed to create more than 7 billion people. He didn't create the sun, the moon, the stars, the animals, plants, trees and flowers, and then decide, "Okay, let me create man." No. The Master Craftsman planned everything ahead of time. He created the birds, the animals, and the colorful flowers as part of the magnificent environment that He prepared for you to enjoy. 1 Timothy 6:17 says that God richly provides us with everything for our enjoyment.

Before God created you, He created an environment for you to thrive in. He created rushing rivers, stunning waterfalls, and vast oceans with a wide array of fish in abundance. He created the majestic mountain ranges, trees of every kind, scenic landscapes, fragrant flowers and plants, gorgeous snow-capped peaks, lush and picturesque green forests and sandy beaches for man to enjoy. God created everything that man could possibly need, but He didn't just stop there. He created much more.

God created the sun and the moon. He didn't just create the sun, moon and stars and stop there. When He creates, He goes big. Psalms 104:2 says He flung the stars into existence like a curtain. Our galaxy contains billions of stars, and there are billions of galaxies. God created everything and then He placed man, the crowning glory of all creation in the midst of what He created, to enjoy the works of His hands.

The motivation behind all of His creation is His amazing grace. God did all this just because He wanted to. Do you realize that without God, there would be no such thing as love? Love is a biblical concept. It all began with God, because God is love. We receive love through the Holy Spirit who is within us (Romans 5:5), and God pours His love through us to touch those around us. God's amazing, boundless love was the motivation behind all of creation. He dreamt and then spoke us into existence to experience His love. God was lavish in everything He did—extreme in everything He created.

Created Uniquely like God

Genesis 1:28 says that God blessed man. The Hebrew word for blessed is 'Barak.' It means an act of adoration such as kneeling. Picture this scene: God has been dreaming about you from eternity[3]. He intricately designed every aspect of you—your physical attributes, your emotions, your intellect, your body structure, and so on. Your DNA has three billion characters. That is replicated in your 75 trillion cells. The fastest computer takes several hours to complete genome sequencing—turning out a complete human DNA profile.[4]

God has created you uniquely in His image, to be compatible with Him, for the purpose of intimacy with Him. We're not just copies of Christ. He uniquely created you to have a unique fingerprint, a unique smile, a unique voice and a uniquely individual face. You are so unique that your DNA, your fingerprint, your voice or your face can identify you. Because the password authentication model is so easily hacked, banks are now introducing voice-recognition authentication. Your voice is incredibly unique! Financial institutions are even introducing face-recognition. No one else has such an amazingly beautiful face quite like yours. You have been uniquely designed for intimacy with your Creator. When you were born, God, who has been thinking of you from eternity, baraked (blessed) you like a father or mother would at the birth of their child. He adores you. That was Adam's first experience when he was created.

Your worship and praise are a natural response to His deep and abiding love. 1 John 4:19, "We love Him because He first loved us."

In Ephesians 1:4 the word 'before' suggests the position and relationship enjoyed by the cream of society in a royal court, by children before their father, by a bride before her bridegroom (The Anchor Bible). In his book 'Church Dogmatics' Karl Barth describes it this way: the 'immediate presence of God to man,' 'the closest proximity of man to God.' It means 'before His scrutinizing gaze.' [4] .I truly believe that if we understood our purpose for existence, our lives would change dramatically. If we fail to understand our purpose, we often think we were created by accident just to take up space until we die, and that belief causes us to run after worthless and dangerous things. We were created for a deep, personal relationship with God, who wants us to live in face-to-face fellowship with Him. It is to that end that God the Father included us in the beautiful relationship that He has with Jesus and the Holy Spirit. God didn't create us to just merely exist. He created us in order to bring us into profound intimacy with Him. Through this intimacy, God's very life and joy flow into us, become ours and overflow to all those with whom we come in contact.

Rom. 6:10, (The New Testament: A Translation in the Language of the People by Charles B. Williams), says this: "For by the death He died He once for all ended His relation to sin, and by the life He now is living He lives in unbroken relation to God."

Jesus assumed the fallen nature of Adam and died to sin. He is now living in uninterrupted fellowship with God. In the same way, we, who are in union with Christ, can live in unbroken fellowship with God that is uninhibited by sin. This became viable because of what happened in His death and resurrection. [4]

Romans 6:5 (The New Testament: An Expanded Translation by Kenneth Wuest) says this: "For in view of the fact that we are those who have become permanently united with Him with respect to the likeness of His death, certainly also we shall be those who as a logical result have become permanently united with Him with respect to the likeness of His resurrection."

God dreamt us up and created us because He wanted to include us in uninterrupted fellowship with Father, Son and Holy Spirit. Now we can effortlessly enjoy that dear, sweet fellowship and live fulfilled in the purpose of our creation.

God has Given You All His Treasures

Ephesians 1:3 says, "He has blessed us with all the treasures of heaven."

Consider this story: A very wealthy man once adopted a poor orphan. The little boy felt unworthy to eat with the rich man's kids. So he hid in the basement and ate table scraps. One day, the caretaker discovered the boy living like a pauper and explained to him that with adoption, he automatically had access to all the privileges of his wealthy father. Though he took some persuasion, the boy shortly began dining at the rich man's table, enjoying the privileges of a son.

Most believers are like that poor orphan boy. The treasures mentioned above in Ephesians 1:3 are the privileges of son-ship. When He planned your creation, God lavishly provided everything that you could possibly need from the day you were born for the rest of your life.

Philippians 4:19 says: "And my God shall supply all your need according to His riches in glory by Christ Jesus," has become a cliché in the charismatic church because we have been taught that we are eligible for this verse only if we give and believe. Believing has been taught as a work—something we must do to receive, but the real truth is that we don't give to receive. Not surprisingly many churches quote Luke 6:38 out of context before the offering is taken in order to motivate givers. The previous seven verses of Luke 6 provide the context for the real meaning of the text. Jesus is saying that if you love, people will love you back, good measure, pressed down and running over. If you do good to others, people will do good to you. If you lend, without expecting anything in return, you will receive financial provision. If you are merciful, you will receive mercy. You won't be judged or condemned if you don't judge or condemn. If you forgive others, others will forgive you. Right after that, we read Luke 6:38. Here Jesus is teaching the principles of the kingdom—not a grab-grab model, but a give-give model. You live a lifestyle of giving in every area—offering love, mercy and forgiveness. You lend out of compassion, expecting nothing in return. A lifestyle of giving will cause you to live a life of great blessing.

Now, all of God's treasures are yours simply by virtue of your identity as His child. You just need to step into His provision that is already yours. You don't give in order to receive. Receiving isn't the motivation for giving. You live a life of giving out of the abundance of who you are in union with Him. You have everything simply because you are one with Him. You give out of the abundance that flows from Him through you to everyone you meet.

Chapter 2: The Incarnation

What actually happened when Jesus came to earth? Jesus was fully God and fully man. I heard this teaching back in the eighties but didn't understand what it really meant.

Jesus wasn't plan B. This is what we have been taught, when Adam sinned, God thought, "Gosh, my plan for man failed." He then scratched His head and thought, "What am I to do now? Let me consult with Jesus and Holy Spirit. I am angry with man because of his outrageous behavior and can't look upon him." In response Jesus said, "Let me take the bullet for man. I will die in the place of man." Jesus then appeased the wrath of God by His sacrificial death on the cross.[2]

That is not what happened. When Adam sinned, God didn't turn His face from him. Rather, Adam and Eve hid themselves from the presence of God because they were ashamed. God came looking for man, saying, "Adam, where are you?" God has been reaching out to man ever since and has never turned His back on man. He came after Abraham saying "Abraham, Abraham!" He came after the Israelites when they were in bondage.

The incredible truth is that God has been reaching out to man ever since and has never turned His back on us.

Colossians 1:21 says, "And you, who once were alienated and enemies in your mind by wicked works, yet now He has reconciled."

It was only in our minds that we were enemies, alienated from God. God wasn't alienated from us. Our sins didn't prevent God from being able to look at us. It was in spite of our sin that He loved us with an everlasting love!

Romans 5:8 says "Christ died for us while we were still

sinners."

The magnificent truth is that Jesus was Plan A. Revelation 13:8 says that Jesus was the Lamb slain from the foundation of the world. God knew before He created man that man would sin, and He already had a plan. He arranged for the ram in the thicket[7] long before it was needed.

Jesus Upholds All Things

Jesus came to earth, fully man, but He was also fully God.

Hebrews 1:3 says, "Who being the brightness of His glory and the express image of His person, and upholding all things by the word of His power."

Jesus is upholding all of creation. He is holding you just as surely as you as you are holding this book or tablet in your hand. He holds you as you drive to work every day. He has held you through all your hard times. Even your next heartbeat depends on Him.

Colossians 1:17 says, "And He is before all things, and in Him all things consist."

All things that were ever created consist in Jesus. The God who holds all things together and in whom all things consist was born as a baby in Bethlehem.

Now Jesus lives for eternity. All of time is contained in Him.

Isaiah 53:5 says "He was wounded for our transgressions, He was bruised for our iniquities."

Seven hundred years before the time of Christ, Isaiah said that He was wounded (past tense) and that He was bruised.

Chapter 2: The Incarnation

Isaiah was speaking about a future event in the past tense. For God, past, present and future are simultaneously present tense.

There is an interesting conversation in John 8:57, "Then the Jews said to Him, 'You are not yet fifty years old, and have You seen Abraham?'" The Jews were asking Jesus how He could have seen Abraham since He was barely fifty years old.

John 8:58 goes on to say: "Jesus said to them, 'Most assuredly, I say to you, before Abraham was, I AM.'" Now, if Jesus had said "Before Abraham was, I was"—that would have been pretty impressive. But He says, "Before Abraham was, I AM." Here's another instance where we see that from God's point of view, the past, present and future are all visible at the same time.

Let me give you an example that will help us understand this better. Every April people in my city, San Antonio celebrate Fiesta. Fiesta has a few beautiful parades. A few years back, I watched one of the parades from the side of the street. At any given point in time, I could see the float in front of me and the floats that were before and behind the float in front of me. I couldn't see the other floats that had already passed by or the floats that were further behind. But when I went up to the top of the Tower of the Americas, I could see all the floats in the parade, from one end of the street to the other. I had a panoramic, 360-degree view of the parade.

In the same way, God has a panoramic, 360-degree view of time. God simultaneously sees your life, your father's life, your grandfather's life, all the way to Moses' life, Abraham's life and Adam's life. He also sees the lives of all your descendants.

All of your existence is contained in Him. Your past, present and future are contained in Him. All of time and all of existence were in Him when the eternal God lived as a human being on earth. When Jesus was born, your entire existence—from the time you were born until the day you die were contained in Him. Jesus didn't just come as a man. He came representing mankind, more completely than any other man ever possibly could. Jesus came to earth as mankind. He represented mankind more completely than Gandhi represented India, more completely than Nelson Mandela represented the oppressed people of South Africa and more completely than Martin Luther King represented the African-Americans in the United States of America. Jesus came as the ultimate representative of mankind. All of your time and all of your existence were in Him while He was here on earth.[a]

Jesus Was You

Jesus entered your very existence. When this Word becomes flesh, it means that whatever you have experienced, He experienced. Whatever you experience now, He experiences. Whatever you face in the future, He faces with you. When Jesus lived, you lived. When Jesus repented and was baptized in Luke 3 and Matthew 3, He repented and was baptized on your behalf. When you repented and were baptized, you identified with His repentance and baptism. Even your faith isn't your faith. It is His faith.[8]

Jesus came and blended humanity into Himself. *The Incarnation is God's embrace of humanity*[2]. God's embrace is more wholesome than man's embrace. When God embraces someone, He blends with every cell of his or her being. When Jesus came to earth, He blended with every cell of your being. He became one with you. *The Incarnation was God's act of including humanity into Himself.* The Triune God included you into Himself when He came to earth. The Incarnation was God's act of including you into the glorious fellowship of Father, Son and Holy Spirit.

Christ is God's mind made up about you. God thought

about you before the foundation of the world and created you because He really wanted you. When man strayed from Him, God came in the form of man to get you back. Jesus explained this to us clearly in Luke 15 in His parables of the lost coin, the lost sheep and the wayward son. He came to get us back to Him. The Incarnation took place because God had already made up His mind that He wanted you, no matter what. The Incarnation is divine proof that God wanted you and didn't want to be without you. The only way you can escape the divine embrace is if you whole-heartedly reject the relentless pursuit of the divine Romancer.

The Ultimate Mediator

1 Timothy 2:5 tells us: "There is one God and one Mediator between God and men, the man Christ Jesus."

Jesus was the mediator between God and man. Most of us understand a mediator to be a third-party mediator who mediates a dispute between two opposing parties, to bring a resolution or settlement. Jesus Christ wasn't a third-party mediator. He was simultaneously God and Man in the person of Jesus Christ.[10]

In the person of Jesus, as God, He is reconciling and embracing humanity, and as man, is reconciled and responds to His embrace. In the person of Jesus, as God, He is judging man and as man, He is accepting that judgment. As God, Jesus demands obedience and as man, He is perfectly obedient to that demand. He was perfectly obedient even unto death. Philippians 2:8 says, "He humbled Himself and became obedient to the point of death, even the death of the cross."[11]

The Old Covenant was between God and man. God was on one side of the covenant, requiring obedience. No man could meet the obedience requirements of the Old Covenant.

The New Covenant was between God on one side of the covenant and God as man on the other side of the covenant. Jesus fulfilled man's side of the covenant in the Incarnation. Man partakes of the covenant in and through Christ.

When He came to earth Jesus embraced the existence of every person who ever lived and every person who will ever live. We read in 2 Corinthians 5:14 that one died for all and therefore all died. When Jesus died, every member of the human race died. The death of Jesus was the death of the entire creation. You may think, "That's absurd. How can all of creation die with just one man?" Well, can you believe that God created the sun, moon, stars, mountains, plants, trees, flowers and creatures? You believe that because you have been taught that from the time you were born. But you may not have heard the plan of God for the salvation of man as I have described it. If you can believe that God is the Creator of all things, it shouldn't be hard to believe that He could also re-create and restore all things. How else would you account for the fact that Jesus bore all your sins and died for you? Just think about it for a moment: Wouldn't it be just as easy to re-create something as to create it? In God's wisdom, this was His plan from before the foundation of the world.

Jesus Undid What Adam Did

John 1: 14 tells us that the Word became flesh. It would have been most logical for John to say that the Word became man. But he deliberately chose the word 'flesh' instead of the word 'man'. Flesh is the basest attribute of man. Flesh is where temptation thrives and where sin is manifested—the arena of temptations and trials[5]. Even though Jesus was fully God in His incarnation, Philippians 2:6-8 says that Jesus laid aside His divine abilities, which allowed Him to be fully God, yet fully man, to live here on earth as you, and experience all the weaknesses and temptations of human nature. Jesus assumed Adam's fallen nature with all its accompanying struggles.

Jesus fully identified with fallen man, and was subject to all the struggles and temptations of the human nature, yet He remained sinless. Hebrews 4:15 says, "For we do not have a High Priest who cannot sympathize with our weaknesses, but was in all points tempted as we are, yet without sin."

1 Corinthians 15:45 tells us that Christ was the last Adam. The obedience of Christ undid all the effects of the fall of Adam. When I was a computer programmer in the 1990s, I developed the 'Undo' feature in several of my applications. In computers with the Windows operating system, 'Control Z' causes an undo of your most recent action. Jesus did a 'Control Z' of Adam. Adam's fall brought man into bondage. The acts of Jesus restored the liberty, life and freedom that God had originally envisioned for man. Christ restored you to your original design. You are now the perfect man[12] created in the image and likeness of the Son of God! Christ was the last Adam: the last man who had Adam's fallen nature. Mankind does not have Adam's fallen sin nature any more. We only have the nature of God.[5]

We have been re-created in His image and likeness. Some of us know this truth and are walking in it. It is our responsibility to share this truth: the almost-too-good-to-be-true news with those who don't know it, so that they too, can benefit from this amazing reality. We need to help everyone realize that they don't have Adam's sinful nature and that they have the nature of God.

Psalm 17:15 (Young's Literal Translation) says this; "I in righteousness see thy face. I am satisfied in awaking with thy form." This is a picture of the act of creation in Genesis 1:26-28. This verse is also a prophetic picture of what happened to you when you died with Jesus and rose with Him as a new creation.

You are a New Creation, Just Like Jesus

When Jesus rose from the dead, you—a brand new creation rose with Him. 2 Corinthians 5:17 says this: "Therefore, if anyone is in Christ, he is a new creation; old things have passed away; behold, all things have become new."

The word for 'new' is the Greek word. *Kainos* means new in quality and new in kind. *Kainos* means superior to what we were in our previous, degenerate state.

This scripture says that we are a new creation and that the old person we were before Christ died and was raised again is extinct. We are part of a new order. Christ destroyed corrupt humanity on the cross. When He rose from the dead, we were created as new creatures with His image.[13]

The old creation and the new creation are not two parts or natures of a person. The old creation was replaced by the new creation when Jesus died and rose again. The new creation is in the image and likeness of the Son of Man. The new creation and the old creation don't co-exist within us. The old nature was replaced by the new nature. Adam is no longer our model. Christ is our model. We don't have the nature of Adam. We have the nature of Christ.[4]

In Christ we are a new creation. Galatians 2:20 tells us that we were crucified with Christ and no longer live, but Christ lives in us.

The Divine Reversal

Christ is referred to as the last Adam in 1 Corinthians 15:45. Every person in every denomination of the church believes that when Adam sinned, we were included and became recipients of the sin nature. However, a large portion of the church doesn't believe that every person was included in the act of reconciliation with Christ[14], and has now received the gift of righteousness and Christ's righteous nature[15].

Romans 5:17 tells us: "For if by the one man's offense death reigned through the one, much more those who receive abundance of grace and of the gift of righteousness will reign in life through the one, Jesus Christ."

We tend to believe that Adam's sinful act was more powerful than God's act of death and resurrection! But it's actually the other way around. Jesus reversed all the negative effects of Adam's sin. Through the death and resurrection of Jesus Christ, we experience divine reversal!

Romans 5:19, 20 says this: "For as by one man's disobedience many were made sinners, so also by one Man's obedience many will be made righteous. Moreover the law entered that the offense might abound. But where sin abounded, grace abounded much more."

This clearly defines God's grace. If Adam's act was able to give man the sin nature (*hamartia* in Greek), how much more would God's grace give us His righteous nature? Folks, just from this scripture, it's clear that you have the nature of God!

When we came to Christ, we entered into a new world. In this new *kainos* world, we don't live with the old, sinful nature of Adam. We have been recreated in His divine image.

Romans 13:14 (Mirror Bible)[1] says this "By being fully clothed in Christ makes it impossible for the flesh to even imagine to find any further expression or fulfillment in lust. Jesus is Lord of your life. "

What Does This Mean for You?

It means we are now dead to sin. The Greek word for sin, *hamartia*, is translated forty-four times as a noun (person, place or thing) and six times as an action verb (*hamartano*) in the New Testament. The church has overwhelmingly interpreted sin as an action and uses it as a verb in most of its teachings. But Paul did not primarily teach about sin as an action. He is talking about your sin nature. Jesus didn't come to erase your sin actions. He came and assumed every man's sin nature and died. When He died, every man's sin nature died. No man has a sin nature any more. You may be thinking, "That is ludicrous! Then why are people sinning?" That is because they still believe they have a sin nature. Everything in the kingdom is received by faith. You are saved by faith, healed by faith, delivered by faith: faith in the finished work of Jesus. To reiterate, according to Galatians 2:20 (Darby), Philippians 3:9 and Mark 11:22, it is not your faith, but the faith of God.

Did Father Forsake Jesus on the Cross?

In the chapter on Creation, I mentioned that for eternity, Father, Son and Holy Spirit had this beautiful relationship of love filled with joy. The Triune God created you, me and all of humanity to include us in this beautiful fellowship to share with us everything that they have with us. They have always maintained this fellowship between them. This fellowship has never been broken even for a moment at any time. You may be thinking, "How about on the cross when Jesus said 'My God, My God, why have You forsaken Me?'" Well, as explained in this chapter on the Incarnation, Jesus came to earth as your representative. He came to earth as the representative of mankind. Jesus lived your life. He experienced everything that you have ever experienced or will experience. As we have already learned, when He died, you died[16]. When He hung on the cross, you hung on the cross. When Jesus said, "My God, My God, why have You forsaken Me?" He said that on your behalf—on behalf of mankind. God did not forsake Jesus when He hung on the cross because He couldn't look upon sin the way we've been taught every Good Friday. Jesus was crying your cry of desperation when you feel forsaken, when you feel that no one cares for you, in your times of trouble when there is no one by your side and you feel helpless and hopeless.[5]

Jesus was quoting Psalm 22. Even back in Jesus' day the Jews memorized some of the popular Psalms and recited them in the synagogue. Psalm 22 was their key messianic psalm. Everyone knew Psalm 22. When Jesus quoted the first verse of the Psalm, the rest of the Psalm automatically went through their minds. It would be just like if I sang the first verse of a famous worship song or hymn like 'Lord, I Lift Your Name on High.' You would automatically sing the next line, 'Lord, I love to sing your praises.' This is because everyone who has been to church in the last twenty-five years has sung this song on multiple occasions and knows this song.

David wrote Psalm 22 prophetically to describe the gory details of the passion of Christ. Jesus was so terribly battered and bruised that He had no strength to get past the first verse. He didn't finish reciting Psalm 22, which was a picture of His crucifixion; rather He fulfilled that psalm. Now, I won't go into the details of every verse in the psalm. But I would like to take you to the end of the Psalm. In verse 24, the Word says, "For he has not despised nor abhorred the affliction of the afflicted; nor has he hidden his face from him; But when he cried to him, he heard."

Psalm 22:24 says that God heard when Jesus cried out "My God, My God, why have you forsaken Me?" on the cross on your behalf. He stooped down and embraced you and died your death.

Romans 5:2 (Mirror Bible)[1] says: "Jesus is God's grace embrace of the entire human race. So here we are, standing tall in the joyful bliss of our redeemed innocence!"

Ah, the amazing love of our wonderful Savior!

God does not forsake anyone. In Hebrews 13:5 He says, "I will never leave you nor forsake you." The Father has never forsaken anyone and never will. He did not forsake Jesus on the cross. 2 Corinthians 5:19 says this: "The Father was in Christ reconciling the world to Himself." The Shack by Paul W. Young is the best book that I've ever read. In this book, Paul Young describes Papa as having nails in His hands.[17] The Father was with Jesus on the cross. Doesn't this revelation just thrill your heart? In the same way, Father, Jesus and Holy Spirit are with you and in you always, every moment of every day of your life, even during your times of greatest difficulty. This was God's plan from eternity.

To review: God's plan from eternity was to include you in the beautiful fellowship of extravagant love and inexpressible joy that has existed between Father, Jesus and Holy Spirit from eternity. I have just explained to you how He did it. You are now in that glorious fellowship every moment of every day, united with Him and inseparable from Him. He knows your every thought. Psalm 139:4 says that before a word is on your lips, He knows it.

Song of Solomon 8:3 tells us: "His left hand is under my head, and His right hand embraces me." This is one of my favorite scriptures. He is your next heartbeat. He is as close to you as close can be, always and forever. This is how He designed it. He accomplished His design all by Himself without help from anybody through His acts of creation[18] and re-creation[19].

Song of Solomon 8:6 says this: "Set me as a seal upon

your heart." That is what He has done to you.

Purpose of Creation Revisited

Now let's look at the second reason you were created. We saw in the chapter on Creation that the first purpose was to include you in the fellowship of Father, Jesus and Holy Spirit. You were created for the purpose of a life of continual intimacy with God.

For whom did God create the world and everything in it? We read in Colossians 1:16 that all things were made through Him and for Him. God created everything for Himself.

We also read in 1Timothy 2:5 that there is one God and one Mediator between God and men, the Man Christ Jesus.

This verse was written decades after Christ's life on earth and refers to Him as 'Man'. Christ is still a Man seated at the right hand of God[21]. Christ is fully God and fully Man.

Now He didn't create this beautiful world and go off to live in heaven and watch us from there as Greek mythology would lead us to believe. He created you so that He could include you in His circle of intimacy. He put you in this world so that He could enjoy the world with you and through you, in intimate fellowship with you.

He loves you so much that He doesn't want to live without you. So He designed you to be compatible with Him, in His image. He created you to be just like Him, so that He could come and make His home in you forever! He created you—a perfect vessel in whom He could make His home forever. He is comfortable in you.

Earlier, we saw that the Creator doesn't need creation to

exist. He existed from eternity before creation. But God decided that He didn't want to be God without man. The only way God wanted to be God was with man and as a Man. He has been God with man through the centuries. Man created all the great innovations and works of art together with God. Some great innovators knew that they created their inventions with God. Others thought that they created their inventions themselves. But in reality, God does all of creation. The earth He has given to the sons of men. But God has united Himself with man and has taken creation to another level by creating with man and through man.

The Great Dance

C Baxter Kruger has a great book called the Great Dance. The Great Dance is you, Father, Son and Holy Spirit swirling around together, enjoying your abundant life here on earth. Kruger mentions that C.S. Lewis called it the Dance.[6] Here are a few examples of the Great Dance.

I make my home in Texas. Today is March 23rd. It is a beautiful spring day and the spring flowers are in bloom. When I walk outside and admire the beautiful wild flowers, I am admiring the beauty of His handiwork, united with Him, in a position of intimacy with Him. Jesus, the Father, Holy Spirit and I enjoy the beautiful Texas blue bonnet patches together. Folks, doesn't this all make such perfect sense? Everything falls into place so beautifully when we look at it this way.

Not long ago I visited the vegetable market at 6 a.m. on a cool December morning in Bangalore, India as part of my early morning workout during a ministry trip. I was just awestruck by how God so generously provided tomatoes, potatoes, onions and other vegetables for such a massive city. When I walked back to my hotel room, the smell of coconut and tomato curries wafted through the cool morning breeze to me, stimulating my appetite. God was right there in every person who was cooking, enjoying the smell with them and with me. He was also there, enjoying the delicious Indian breakfast with each family.

Today is May 16th. Two days back, as I was walking out of my room to go to the Holy Ghost explosion to preach, I saw the Great Dance being played out by little children. They were playing hide and seek. One of the kids was blindfolded, trying to spot the other kids. They were all so happy. Father, Son, Holy Spirit and each of the kids were playing hide and seek.

Every day when I walk out of my bedroom at home in San Antonio Texas, I witness the Great Dance being played by my wife Selvi, my daughter Priya and my grand-daughter Selah. Father, Son, Holy Spirit, Selvi, Priya and Selah spend hours enjoying each other and the simple things of life, as Selah plays with her toys and is in ecstasy.

Because of our dualistic mindset, we can't imagine that a spiritual God would be interested in these mundane activities of the flesh. God is right here with every man, woman and child in every country on earth. His name is Immanuel. Jesus wasn't Immanuel only when He lived on earth. He is Immanuel right here and right now!

We have been taught that we were born with Adam's sinful nature and that God is slowly molding us into His image. Every church has its own interpretation of what Jesus is like, with everyone trying to become this patient, gentle, mature stereotype that we have created. You have been uniquely created just like Jesus to live in freedom with Him every day of your life, so be free! Enjoy your life of freedom with Jesus instead of living in bondage, trying to be what some church has said you should be!

Today is May 15th. Yesterday I preached my fourth

message at Berachah Prophetic Ministries first five-day Holy Ghost Explosion. It has been incredible. I am in ecstasy. On the night of the third day, everyone was drunk in the Spirit, like they had drunk a bottle of wine each. More than a 1000 hungry people were acting like fools. After sister Benita Francis spoke, there was an outpouring of joy. Some were laughing uncontrollably, like they had been struck with a huge bolt of electricity. Some of the people were rolling on the floor. I have been to the Pensacola revival. I have attended many conferences and meetings in Toronto revival churches. I attended all 40 days of Rodney Howard Browne's meetings in the 90s in Florida a couple of times. I have never been in a place where the presence of God was as strong as it is in the meetings here in India. I can't imagine that heaven could be better than what I am experiencing now. Prophet Ezekiah Francis has trained more than 40000 people in his 30-90 day schools. They are scattered all over India. Many of them are now pastors of large churches. Many of them are now leading evangelists in India. Many of them have powerful healing ministries.

Yesterday morning, when I shared this truth about Jesus being the last Adam and the reversal of the Adamic nature, a pastor came up to me and said he teaches that children are born with the sinful nature. He asked me how children seem to naturally be inclined to sin. I explained to him about how God has created us as free people with the freedom of choice. When we raise our children in the grace-law-mixture-based model, sin raises its ugly head because sin is the strength of the law. When we raise our kids in this model, it may appear that they are inclined to sin. The Old Testament model is law and judgment based where we punish our children. Instead, we can raise children in the New Testament grace-based model. We speak to their identity and help them look into the mirror of who they are. We repeatedly show them who they are. They will live out of their true identity and will be less inclined to sin. When they are adamant about something, we distract them towards something that is more appealing, rather than tell them not to do something. We can nurture them to grow in the image of Christ.

Your life is here on earth. It's the reason you're here. In 2 Corinthians 3:3 Paul said that we are living epistles. You were created for greatness. You write history with your life. So don't worry that you may not be in God's plan, because your life on earth is His plan for you. What you do in your life, together with God is His plan for you.

What a privilege to be one with Him! That was His prayer in John 17:21 "That they all may be one, as You, Father, are in me, and I in You; that they also may be one in us." Jesus prayed this prayer and fulfilled it in His death and resurrection by uniting Himself with us! He created you to include you in the beautiful fellowship of overflowing, abundant love and joy that the Father, Jesus and Holy Spirit have been enjoying from eternity. Then He created this beautiful world, put you in it and came to enjoy His creation with you and through you from the day you were born for eternity.

When I go on my preaching trips, my wife Selvi and I tell each other, "Honey, you may be away in a distant place, but I am in you." But we are not really in each other. The love of God is even greater than the love of a couple! A couple can get pretty close to each other, but your relationship with God is so close that you are in Him and He is in you! Isn't that amazing?

Chapter 3: God is Full of Grace

Aah! What would we do and where would we be without the grace of God! The gospel of Jesus Christ is a message of His grace. Our God does everything by His grace. He goes over and above anything we could dream or imagine in His love, provision and care of us. Just looking around us we find overwhelming evidence of the lavish abundance and perfection with which He has created everything.

Galatians 1:6 tells us: "I marvel that you are turning away from grace to a different gospel."

God is abundant in mercy, who gives us abundant life and loves us with an overwhelming, everlasting love. Jesus came for the purpose of giving you life that you might have it abundantly.

Paul said in Galatians 3:2-3: "This only I want to learn from you: Did you receive the Spirit by the works of the law, or by the hearing of faith? Are you so foolish? Having begun in the Spirit, are you now being made perfect by the flesh?"

Grace Doesn't Mix with Works

Grace isn't meant to be mixed with works. In fact, grace and works don't mix any better than oil and water. Grace and works are polar opposites. The main difference between the Old and New Covenants is that the Old Covenant was based on works and the New Covenant is based on grace. John 1:17 says this: "For the law was given through Moses; grace and truth came through Jesus Christ."

God gives grace freely over and above what we deserve or could ever obtain on our own. The problem is that the church has been trying to earn God's favor and blessings. However

Chapter 3: God is Full of Grace

God's favor and blessings are already ours for the taking[1]. Instead of walking in His favor and blessings, we have been trying to please God with our good behavior and works, putting the cart before the horse. Ironically, we're trying to earn what God has already given us for free. John Crowder has a wonderful message called 'Freedom from God-pleasing'. God is already pleased with you in Christ.

Matthew 17:5 says: "This is My beloved Son, in whom I am well pleased." Ephesians 1:6 goes on to say: "We are accepted in the beloved." When you recognize and live according to your true identity, your walk will be continually pleasing to Him—as a natural fruit of your fellowship with Him.

God in Creation

Our God is not a God of the ordinary. Think about it! God went overboard with everything He did. He created billions of galaxies, with billions of stars in each galaxy. Wouldn't a single galaxy with a few stars have been enough? He created more than 7 billion people, and 32,000 species of fish. Wouldn't you consider that a little overboard? Well, consider this: there are 116,500 species of snails!—those sluggish creatures that crawl back into their shells at the slightest provocation. Wouldn't a couple of species of snails have been enough?

Recently I watched a show about Madagascar. Most of the animal species that are found there are found nowhere else on earth. After God created the earth in all its splendor and majesty, I think He probably had this little pet side project and created a little fantasy garden, the island of Madagascar, on which to lavish His incredible creativity, as an after-thought. One animal genus, the lemur, is found only in Madagascar, and there are a remarkable 100 species of lemurs!

Everything about God is extreme. His love is without

height or depth or length or width. His peace far surpasses understanding. His joy is unspeakable. His mercy and kindness are everlasting. Genesis 21:33 tells us that His name is Everlasting God. You or I may choose to die protecting our nation, but He died so that *no one* should perish[3]. His love is so amazing that He lived and died for everyone in the world. In the same way, His grace is amazing. Grace is what God does without any assistance from anyone just because He wants to. Psalm 103:3 says "Who forgives all your iniquities, who heals all your diseases." Now, that really is extreme! You've probably heard people say, "You should never use the word 'all.' You should never say 'never.' You should qualify your statements and not be so inclusive and not be so inclusive." Not my God. He forgives all! He heals all!

Grace and Forgiveness

You and I may forgive some people of some sins, but His amazing grace forgives everyone in the whole wide world that ever existed of all their sins, past, present and future. That is my God. Psalm 103:12 says: "As far as the east is from the west, so far has He removed our transgressions from us." He didn't just throw our sins over His shoulder. He obliterated even the memory of them. But traditional thinking wants us to go fishing for them, to feel guilty and miserable over them, to brood over them and feel worthless. Instead I believe we should just thank God for His forgiveness and rejoice in His mercy and grace that He has so freely given us. When I finally grasped the revelation of this truth, I told my wife, "Honey, I forgive you of everything that you are ever going to do to me." I shared this when I was teaching at a ministry school. One man who was sitting there with his wife immediately responded, "If I did that, my wife would do whatever she wanted." Yet I was thinking—*That's the whole point.* Some of us tend to want to control people in our relationships to make them behave the way we want them to.

Galatians 5:1 (NIV) says this: "It is for freedom that Christ has set us free."

When God created man, He created him with complete and unlimited freedom, to such a degree that man could choose to go to hell if he so desired. Ironically, real love can only originate from free choice that can't be coerced. In fact, God created man to be the object of His love, for the primary purpose of experiencing His love and to love other human beings in return. The reality is that our relationships would be miraculously enhanced if we set others free, and refused to impose our ideas on them. Relationships aren't nearly as successful if there is an element of control in them.

All our sins were forgiven when Jesus died on the cross. 1 John 1:7 and 1:9 talk about this. 1 John 1:9 talks about confessing our sins. This doesn't mean we have to mourn or do penance of any kind in order for God to forgive us. We simply come to Him boldly as beloved children and discuss our weaknesses with Him frankly and openly, knowing that we do not have a High Priest who cannot sympathize with our weaknesses, but was in all *points* tempted as *we are, yet* without sin[4].

God Doesn't Think the Way We Do

Our misunderstanding of grace stems from doctrines of penance that originated in the Middle Ages. We live in a world where everything is based on works and judgment. When you do something worthy of praise, you deserve a reward; when you do something bad, you deserve punishment. So we project that thinking back on God. We have trouble forgiving people. Even if we do forgive, our capacity to forgive is severely limited. So we can't comprehend a God with an unlimited capacity to forgive. We as humans simply can't imagine a God who would let people go scot-free when they sin. We think people deserve to be punished, even though God has based the entire New Covenant on mercy and grace.

Hebrews 8:12 says, "For I will be merciful to their unrighteousness, and their sins and their lawless deeds I will remember no more."

In Eastern cultures, it is generally thought that if you forgive others, you encourage them to repeat their harmful behaviors. However, the basis of Christianity is forgiveness that ultimately brings freedom. Forgiveness was God's idea from the outset. Do you know how God defeats His enemies? He does it by forgiving them and making them His friends. God's ways are clearly not like our ways.

Isaiah 55:8-9 says this: "For my thoughts *are* not your thoughts, nor *are* your ways my ways," says the Lord. "For *as* the heavens are higher than the earth, so are my ways higher than your ways, and my thoughts than your thoughts."

The Pharisee in Luke 7 didn't like the fact that Jesus quickly forgave a woman of questionable reputation. Jesus turned and told him outright that she was forgiven—in other words He would never again hold her past against her. To the Pharisee it was like adding insult to injury: he was irate that the woman was even in his house, let alone that she was kissing Jesus' feet in gratitude. But Jesus wasn't thinking, "If I forgive this woman, she'll go right out and sin again." The Pharisee didn't think Jesus should let the sinful woman touch Him. But Jesus not only accepted her touch, He relished her kisses on His feet. Responding to the anger of the Pharisee, Jesus said the woman hadn't once *stopped* kissing His feet, whereas the Pharisee hadn't given Him a single kiss.

1 Samuel 16:7 says, "God does not see as a man sees.

Man looks at the outward appearance, but God looks at the heart."

Friend of Sinners

Much of our Churchianity is based on outward appearances, which lead us into bondage. That's why we have so much furor over preachers who preach freedom and hope. Perhaps you've heard Jesus called a friend of sinners. In spite of what others thought, He hobnobbed with prostitutes and tax collectors, the worst sinners of His day. The Pharisees were infuriated about this and asked Him about it. Jesus said in Matthew 9:12: "Those who are well have no need of a physician, but those who are sick."

How many of our churches would even allow a prostitute or a gay person to enter our doors? We would probably tell them that they would be welcome after they abandoned their evil ways. However, we need to understand that most people imprisoned by addictions are in bondage from which they cannot escape on their own. Only God can set them free. If people could free themselves of their addictions on their own, they wouldn't need God in the first place.

The truth is that without God it is difficult, if not impossible to overcome addictions and sinful practices. And in exactly the same way Jesus did, it's our responsibility to share God's love and His delivering power with those in desperate need, in order to set them free. Instead, our churches are close-knit cliques, proud of how holy we are, looking down our sanctimonious noses at those wretched sinners. For all intents and purposes, our church doors are closed and locked against those in need. Jesus had an open-door policy. Sinners were inexplicably drawn to Him and flocked to Him. We need more people like Mother Theresa and Heidi Baker filled with the love of Jesus, who embrace desperately needy people without judging them.

In the Old Testament, when a leper touched you, you became unclean. In the New Testament, Jesus touched the leper, and the leper was cleansed. We must abandon our Old Testament mindset that says we are defiled if we associate with sinners. In the chapter called 'Living under an Open Heaven' we will learn that it is our mandate to bring heaven to earth. The church is not a club for saints, which is what we have made it. The church is a hospital for those who are hurting and in bondage.

Saul (who later became Paul) was a Pharisee who hated believers who lived in freedom, because it messed with his preconceived religious paradigm. He was angered by this new religion where people were forgiving others and loving their neighbors. So he went on a killing spree, on a mission to exterminate Christians. Jesus told Saul, "Saul, you are kicking against the goads. I am Jesus whom you are persecuting." We don't want to be caught in the wrong camp like Saul or the Pharisee.

Is God Angry and Judgmental?

Many of us have a mistaken notion that God is a cranky old, nitpicking judge in heaven waiting with a big stick to judge us and beat us up for every little failure. This kind of thinking is widely prevalent in the church today. However, the truth is quite the opposite. God has already judged Jesus for all our sins. So He isn't going to judge us again for the same sins. We're off the hook! Jesus bore all your sins once and for all, and took all your punishment, so you wouldn't have to. This is Gospel 101, and it should cause us to jump and shout for joy!

The problem is, we're a judgmental people who have created a judgmental God in our image. We are limited in our ability to forgive. We project this on God, and paint Him as someone who can only forgive to a certain degree, which then excuses us when we behave that way. If we believe that God is judgmental, we too will be judgmental. If we think God is an angry God, we will be angry people, which is exactly the opposite of what God desires. Genesis 1:26 says we have been created in God's image, which means we are to be as loving as He is, filled with grace. Romans 5:20 says this: "Moreover the law entered that the offense might abound. But where sin abounded, grace abounded much more."

The Greek word for 'abounded much more' in verse 20 is *hyperperisseuo,* which means to increase all the more, exceed bounds, overflow to super-abound; to abound still more. We are to be fanatical forgivers, who soar in grace and dispense it freely and abundantly! In Matthew 5, Jesus tells us not to be judgmental. These truths have released me into a freedom that is bringing me boundless joy. Judging people and harboring unforgiveness will actually work against you, to keep you in bondage and steal your joy.

God's Judgment

Jesus said in John 5: 22, "For the Father judges no one, but has committed all judgment to the Son." We have characterized God as an angry judge sitting in an empty courtroom before the world was created. We think He created man in order to have someone to judge and punish. But in John 5:22 Jesus clearly tells us that the Father judges no one. So you may say, "True, but He says the Son will judge us."

Jesus said again in John 12:31-33, "Now is the judgment of this world; now the ruler of this world will be cast out. And I, if I am lifted up from the earth, will draw all peoples to Myself. This He said, signifying by what death He would die." When Jesus referred to that specific point in history He was talking about the judgment of the world coming upon Him on the cross. In verse 32, the word 'peoples' is in italics. This signifies that that the word wasn't in the original translation, and the translators added it because that's how they interpreted that verse. The literal Greek says 'draw this to myself.' This verse should read "And I, if I am lifted up from the earth, will draw this to Myself." So what is He referring to when He uses the word 'this'? Let's consider this verse in context. The previous verse talks about the judgment of this world, so this verse should mean that Jesus would draw all judgment to Himself. Or better still, He will draw all judgment of all peoples to Himself. Jesus took our judgment on our behalf, so that we would not be judged. Hallelujah!

The point I'm trying to make here is that we don't need to fear judgment. Jesus has already borne our judgment once and for all in order to set us free. Our God came to earth in order to bear not just some, but *all* our judgment! Now you may ask, "Do you mean that there is no more judgment?" That was God's final judgment of the world for all eternity; all other judgment is based on God's judgment of man that fell upon Jesus, allowing God to judge man innocent and set him free. Romans 5:8-9 (Mirror Bible)[5] says: "Herein is the extremity of God's love gift: mankind was rotten to the core when Christ died their death. If God could love us that much when we were ungodly and guilty, how much more are we free to realize His love now that we are declared innocent by his blood?"

Now I know the Bible tells us about the White Throne Judgment and the Judgment Seat of Christ. Man will be judged corresponding to his response to the judgment of God on Jesus more than 2,000 years ago. They are man's judgment that falls upon himself based on whether or not he chose to believe/accept/receive/identify with God's judgment upon

Jesus that declared man to be innocent.

Jesus Came to be Judged on Our Behalf

John 3:17 (NASB) says: "For God did not send the Son into the world to judge the world, but that the world might be saved through Him." Jesus didn't come to judge us. He came to save us. All these years, we've had it backward. How can anyone not rejoice and get excited about such an incredible truth! It's very freeing—in fact, I felt like a bird let out of a tiny, stifling cage when I finally understood that there's no old man up there waiting to beat us up for all our mistakes! It should bring us so much joy! How can anyone be against a truth that brings such inspiring hope!

Romans 5:10[5] (Mirror Bible) goes on to say: "Our hostility and indifference toward God did not reduce his love for us. He saw equal value in us when he exchanged the life of his Son for ours."

In John 12:47-48 Jesus said: "And if anyone hears My words and does not believe, I do not judge him; for I did not come to judge the world but to save the world. He who rejects Me, and does not receive My words, has that which judges him—the word that I have spoken will judge him in the *last day*" (Emphasis mine).

Please note that He doesn't say 'in the last days.' He says 'in the last *day*.' It is a one-time judgment. We have incorrectly interpreted it to mean an ongoing judgment that God dispenses to us on a daily basis for all our actions.

When a judge judges someone, his options are either guilty or innocent. We use the word judge in our everyday parlance to mean 'make a decision' or 'determine.' But in church, we get stupid, and change our understanding of the word 'judgment' to always mean 'punishment.' The Greek words for judgment and punishment are in no way related. On the last day (singular), He will judge you based on whether you believe that Jesus is your Savior. He isn't judging you every day of your life and rewarding you on a day-to-day basis based on your good or bad works. We must be delivered from this way of thinking, because this will absolutely ruin us and keep us in bondage.

For many years, if my wife or kids got sick, I would examine myself for what I might have done wrong, and what I could do better to improve my family's health. We can't walk in God's supernatural, divine health, or any of His blessings with this kind of mindset. *We are healed, not based on what we do, but based on what He did on the cross.* This is the key to walking in divine healing. We need to change our mindset from a works-based thinking to a grace-based thinking in order to tap into any of God's blessings.

Isaiah 53:5 says, "But He was wounded for our transgressions, He was bruised for our iniquities; the chastisement for our peace was upon Him, and by His stripes we are healed."

The judgment of God is a vast subject. I have just touched on a few passages of scripture. A great number of Scripture verses have been translated incorrectly in many popular translations. This has the church reeling under a terrible, erroneous misunderstanding of God's judgment.

Chapter 4: Grace and Sin

We are not healed by our good works or obedience, but simply by His stripes. Yet oddly enough if something bad happens, we immediately conclude that we must have done something wrong and are being punished. In the same way, on any given day, if we've failed to live up to some nebulous holy standard of our own making, we feel unworthy to be blessed. So we rob ourselves of the blessings the Lord has already set apart for us.

Ephesians 1:3 says this: "Blessed be the God and Father of our Lord Jesus Christ, who has blessed us with every spiritual blessing in the heavenlies in Christ."

God provides for us and protects us, not based on our works, but based on His grace, because of His intense love for us and because He wants to bless us and keep on blessing us. When we live in this revelation, we can constantly live in His protection, provision and healing. If, on the other hand, on some days we think we deserve His blessings, and on others we don't, then we won't be able to believe for the automatic protection and provision that are already ours. How tragic!

1 Timothy 6:17 tells us that God gives us richly all things to enjoy. The thinking that we don't deserve His goodness is what deprives us of His blessings. We don't think we are worthy of His goodness and His blessings. Well, Jesus thought we were worthy. This truth is clearly articulated in Luke 15 in the parables of the lost coin, the lost sheep and the wayward son. Jesus valued you so highly that He came and died for you! I want you to get this truth deep into your spirit and believe it without doubting, because it will change your very life and bring you new hope and incredible joy and freedom.

Even when we do make a mistake, we can choose to rest

in the grace of God, realizing that we are still pleasing to Him. His love doesn't change depending on our behavior; but based on His purpose and what Jesus has done to get us back to a right relationship with God. If we fail to embrace this mindset, our lives will be like a continuous roller coaster ride, up one day and down the next depending on our perception of our worth. The truth is that we are always pleasing to God just the way we are. Because of His deep and endless love, God wants to constantly protect and provide for us at all times the same way we as parents care deeply about the welfare of our children.

If you have read this far, you either love what I am saying or you're furious. You may be thinking, "The world is already going to hell in a hand-basket. This kind of thinking and teaching will only make it worse."

Our Old Nature is Dead

Jesus didn't come for behavior modification. He changed our very nature; the old nature is dead. He came and rescued us from it.

He embraced you when He lived here on earth. When He died, you died[1]. When He rose, you rose with Him as a new creation. Not just you, but the entire world. All the people in this world are now part of a new creation. You and I know it. However, there are many others who don't. Our responsibility here on earth is to get this truth out: that they are free, just as we are free; they are delivered just as we are delivered. They do have a part to play in identifying with, participating in and living in this relationship with God through Jesus Christ. This is the true gospel of Jesus Christ.

In Acts 20:24 Paul says: "…which I received from the Lord Jesus, to testify to the gospel of the grace of God." The gospel of Jesus is the gospel of the grace of God. Any other message is not the gospel. If you have been hearing or teaching anything else, you have been hearing men's views and teaching your views, which is not at all the gospel.

We just need to help the world realize this truth and recognize that they are free, that they are not in bondage anymore. They are free from sin. If a person is free from something, he doesn't need to live in bondage to it anymore, but he can still choose to live in bondage. Why would I, who am free from sin, live any longer in it? This is exactly what Paul asks in Romans 6:2: "Certainly not! How shall we who died to sin live any longer in it?" You are dead to the world you used to live in, the world of sin, disease, sickness and poverty. Now you abide in a new world that is free from all forms of bondage. God loved you so much that He rescued you from all forms of bondage that man created for himself. He lifted you out of the quagmire of sin and bondage and set you on firm ground, never to be captive again.

The Grace Message and Sin

When Paul taught something similar to what I am teaching in Romans 4 and 5, the natural response was Romans 6:1: "What shall we say then? Shall we continue in sin that grace may abound?" If people are not asking you the question they asked Paul in Romans 6:1, then you're probably not preaching the gospel the way Paul preached it. The fact that people are outraged at our message is proof that we are in good company with Paul and are preaching the gospel the way he preached it. Paul responds to the question from Romans 6:1 in the next verse: "Certainly not! How shall we who died to sin live any longer in it?" There you go! His response was, "That question is absurd! How can we live in something that we have been delivered from?"

How can we, who are holy, righteous and perfect, live in

sin? How can we, who are citizens of heaven, live like the devil? How can we, who are seated in the heavenlies, live in the pits of filth and wretchedness? How can we, who are filled with the glory of God, wallow in the gutters of debauchery and drunken stupor?

Francois du Toit tells us in Romans 6:21 (Mirror Bible)[4] "Sin is the worst thing you could ever do with your life."

You may ask, "But what do you say to those who are still living in sin?" Well, there are some sitting under the preaching that says we have a dual nature, and still live in sin. It is far more likely that you will live in sin if you believe that you have the sin nature and are capable of sin, than if you believe you are the righteousness of God in Christ Jesus—if you believe that you've been created in the image of God, for the purpose of fellowship and intimacy with Him.

Did you know that you don't have the ability to sin? 1 John 3:9 says, "Whoever has been born of God does not sin, for His seed remains in him; and he **cannot** sin, because he has been born of God." The Bible says you cannot sin! You may say, "Well, then why do I still sin?" The word that is translated 'cannot' in this verse is *'no dunamis.'* This means you don't have the power or the ability within yourself to sin. Your new nature doesn't have the capacity to sin.

In fact, the only way you can sin is if you believe a lie of the enemy (from an external source) and act upon it the same way Adam and Eve fell for the same ruse in the Garden. They were created in the image of God, but the devil lied and told them they could become like God if they ate of the forbidden fruit. It was a lie because they were already like God. Genesis 1:26 says Adam was created in the image of God. The devil asked them to do something (eat of the fruit) to become what they already were, and they believed his lie and sinned. The church is still falling for the very same lie of the devil and doing things (works) to become what they already are: righteous, holy and pleasing to God. *This is the great deception.*

Living from Our Identity

If you mistakenly believe you still have the old nature, you give yourself an excuse to sin. The secret to living in freedom is to believe God's Word like it is true. Proverbs 23:7 says: "For as a man thinks in his heart, so is he."

If you think you are a sinner, you'll be a sinner. If you think you are holy and righteous, you will be holy and righteous. I am not talking about mind over matter here. I am talking about God's Word over the enemy's lies. In 2 Corinthians 5:21, Romans 5:9 and a host of other scriptures, the Bible says that you are already righteous. Now I know that Isaiah 64:6 says your righteousness is as filthy rags, and I am not saying that you are righteous by your own works or good deeds—not at all. Jesus became sin that you might become the righteousness of God in Him. A transfer took place on the cross. He took your sins and gave you His righteousness as a gift, because of His great love for you. He took your sinful nature upon himself and died your death so that you could be free. Again, let me reiterate that if you see yourself as righteous, you're more likely to behave that way. If you see yourself as a sinner, you're far more likely to sin.

For example, if you repeatedly tell your kids how bad they are and keep beating them over the head with those words, they will probably live up to your expectations. On the other hand, if you affirm your kids, telling them you believe in them, they will live up to that. I think that God probably well understood that notion, which is why He didn't leave us with our old sin nature and our tendency to sin. Instead He made us righteous, holy and perfect and is now saying, "Be ye perfect" and "Be ye holy." So choose to walk according to your new identity and inheritance. God knew who we are before the foundation of the world. He created us in His image and likeness, *just like Him*. He has faith in His design of you.

Romans 6:19 (Mirror Bible)[4] says: "I want to say it as plainly as possible: you willingly offered your faculties to obey sin, you stained your body with unclean acts and allowed lawlessness to gain supremacy in all of your conduct; in exactly the same way, I now encourage you to present your faculties and person to the supremacy of righteousness to find unrestricted expression in your lifestyle."

In this verse Paul says we have now been transformed and should choose to live out of our righteous nature for the glory of God.

In Romans 6:22 (Mirror Bible)[4] he goes on to say: "A life bonded to God yields the sacred expression of his character, and completes in your experience what life was always meant to be."

This verse talks about the reality of our union with Christ and the result, living in the fullness of life.

God's Word Empowers Us

When Jesus told the paralytic to take up His bed and walk, He wasn't telling him to lift up his pallet and get up in his own strength. The very words of Jesus actually empowered the cripple to get up and walk. When He spoke to the woman caught in the act of adultery He said this: "'Neither do I condemn you; go and sin no more'[2], He wasn't asking her to go in her own strength and sin no more. His words transformed her from the inside out and empowered her to go and sin no more. The Bible says that you are holy and perfect. But perhaps you're thinking, "No, the Bible is saying to be holy, to be perfect, which means that we should work at becoming more holy over time as long as we live."

Holiness is Not Progressive

I love the two illustrations made by John Crowder in his masterpiece *Mystical Union*.[2]

If you take a bottle of 100% pure, drinking water and add a single drop of sewage to it, the purity of the water doesn't reduce to 99%; it is completely polluted—contaminated. In the same way, if you are unfaithful to your spouse one day out of the year, you aren't 99% faithful; you are unfaithful. You're either faithful or you're not. There is no middle ground. Similarly, you are either holy or you are not. You don't gradually improve how holy you are over time. You don't become 80% holy after walking in the way for 40 years. Unfortunately, this is the way the church looks at the subjects of holiness and sanctification. We have been erroneously taught that over time we are gradually purified as we peel away layers of sin, much like we might peel an onion.

The truth is that when God designed you before the foundation of the world, He designed you as a perfect, righteous being in His image. 2 Corinthians 5:21 tells us that Jesus became sin that you might become the righteousness of God in Christ Jesus. When He died, you died. Your old man with its old nature died and is no more.

2 Corinthians 5:14 tells us that if One died for all, then all died. 2 Corinthians 5:17 tells us that when He rose, a new creation came into being, a new creation that is holy, righteous and perfect. That is who you are, because everything and everyone that God created is perfect. God has never created anything that is imperfect. Now, you just need to realize who you are and live accordingly.

The Final State

What you do doesn't determine who you are. Who you are determines what you do. When God created something, He created it in its final state. Isaiah 46:10 says that God declares the end from the beginning.

When God created the first oak tree, He created everything that the oak tree and all its descendants could possibly need. He gave it sunlight, roots, leaves and everything it needed for its nourishment. He also built into it a way to reproduce. Dr. Myles Munroe says that when God created the first oak tree, He didn't just create an oak tree. He created forests of oak trees over several generations. Similarly, when God created man, He created man as righteous, holy and perfect. He created man with everything he could possibly need for his lifetime and for all successive generations. We just need to recognize this truth and walk in it.

2 Peter 1:3 says: "His divine power has given to us all things that pertain to life and godliness." God has given us everything that we need to live.

Ephesians 1:3 says, "He has blessed us with every spiritual blessing in the heavenlies in Christ."

This is God's model for every living creature. Instead, we constantly try to attain what He has already created us to be. In Genesis 1:26, the Bible clearly says that we have been created in God's image. So what do you need to do to become like God? The answer is, 'Nothing.' You don't need to do anything to become like God. You are already like God. Adam's sin separated man from God. 2 Corinthians 5:17 tells us that Jesus restored the image of God to us through His incarnation. You are now in the image of God. You just need to act like it and not try to become something that you already are by your works.

Chapter 4: Grace and Sin

The Consequences of Sin

God will not punish you with pneumonia because you yelled at your spouse. But just because there are no consequences from God on a vertical level, doesn't mean there won't be consequences between you and your wife, on a horizontal level. God has taken care of all your sin, past, present and future.[5] Sin is no longer a problem to God. But sin could be a problem between you and your fellow-human beings, because of the law of sowing and reaping. If you continually yell at your wife, you may break her spirit so that she can no longer tolerate such abuse. And though sin may not be a problem to God, that doesn't mean He approves of it. He hates sin because sin breaks fellowship between Him and you, and hinders you from receiving His provision for you. Sin could also invite sickness and poverty to overtake you, and rob you of blessings He has freely given you because of His love and grace. There are consequences to sin.

God is pleased with you, not because of what you have done, but because of what Jesus has done. That doesn't mean that God can't stand to look at you and that He only looks at Jesus and loves Jesus. He loves you for who you are! Ephesians 1:4 tells us that He has designed you and created you for the very purpose of love before the foundation of the world. Through the act of the Incarnation, Jesus united Himself with you. He has integrated Himself into every part of you. You and He are now one. His righteousness is now your righteousness. Just as you can't saint yourself into His righteousness, you can't sin yourself out of it. You and He are one. You are in the divine embrace.

However, there are consequences to sin, in the same way there are dire consequences when you stick your hand in a fire or jump off the cliff. If you are unfaithful to your spouse, there could be disastrous consequences. Alcoholism and drugs could ruin you and your family. If you slack off at work, you may displease your management.

You are Free from Sin

Paul says in Romans 6:11 (The Message): "From now on, think of it this way: Sin speaks a dead language that means nothing to you; God speaks your mother tongue, and you hang on every word. You are dead to sin and alive to God. That's what Jesus did."

You are a new creation in a new world speaking a new language. You are dead to the old world and the old world is dead to you. You don't recognize, nor can you even hear the enticing whispers of sin any more.

Romans 6:14 (Mirror Bible)[4] says: "Sin was your master while the law was your measure; now grace rules. (The law revealed your slavery to sin, now grace reveals your freedom from it.)"

You are now free from the shackles of sin.

I want to share familiar stories about a man and an eagle that were free, but lived in bondage even after they were set free.

After World War 2 ended, one Japanese soldier remained on an island, hiding in the woods, because he refused to believe the war was over. In fact, he spent an additional twenty years there before he received a letter from his commander telling him it was over and he could go home a free man.

Francois Du Toit wrote a booklet about a captive eagle that wouldn't fly even after she was released. But then, when she saw another eagle flying in the distance, she was finally able to grasp who she was, and flap her wings to soar into freedom.

Many of us are like the Japanese soldier and the eagle.

We don't realize who we are! We don't realize that we are free from sin. The moment we realize our identity, and the fact that we are free from sin, we will rise up out of the bondage, free from the shackles of sin to live life to the fullest.

The Old Dual Nature Model of Living

Let's look at the two models to see how they work. The first is the *Dual Nature Model*, where we believe we have a dual nature: with both the flesh man and the spirit man coexisting inside of us. We are completely convinced that we still have our old sin nature, so we make every effort to crucify and overcome it by the Spirit. And while this is often quite effective, there are times when we fail. Then we go through a cycle of guilt and misery, repenting and praying through until we believe God has finally forgiven us.

While we are in that dungeon of guilt, feeling worthless, we can easily fall into the trap of thinking we're useless and out of fellowship with God, so what difference would it make if we go out and sin again? At a certain point, we muster up enough faith to believe we are forgiven and then repeat the same cycle all over again. Some of us have a little more faith for forgiveness and believe in keeping short accounts with God. Because we feel guilty when we sin we quickly repent and believe we are just as quickly forgiven, until we sin again. The root problem, however, is the same—a mistaken belief that we still have a sin nature. Remember, Proverbs 23:7 says, "For as a man thinks in his heart, so is he."

Holy Spirit and Sin

Part of the issue is that people think the Holy Spirit is convicting them based on their incorrect interpretation of John 16:8-11: "And when He has come, He will convict the world of sin, and of righteousness, and of judgment: of sin, because they do not believe in Me; of righteousness, because I go to My Father and you see Me no more; of judgment, because the ruler of this world is judged."

Here Jesus is talking about Holy Spirit. The traditional but incorrect interpretation is that Holy Spirit convicts you, the believer—of sin. So you think He is convicting you and you dwell in that state of misery, which you believe you rightly deserve. Because you think Holy Spirit is convicting you, you want to yield to Holy Spirit and not resist Him. Can you see the huge deception here? But if you read verse 9 carefully, you will see that Holy Spirit convicts *the world* of sin[5].The phrase 'the world' refers to unbelievers. In verse 10, John clearly says that Holy Spirit convicts you, the believer of *righteousness*.

You are Holy, Righteous and Perfect

Now let's look at the other model, which I will call the Righteousness Model of the true gospel of Jesus Christ. In this model, once you come to a saving knowledge of Jesus, you are holy, righteous and perfect. When you are faced with temptation, Holy Spirit, who dwells in you convicts you, not of sin, but of righteousness (see John 16:10 above). What does that mean? It means the Holy Spirit convinces you that you are righteous, holy and perfect and urges you to do the right thing in accord with who you are. He affirms you and doesn't put you down and make you feel wretched, guilty or miserable. Since you know you are holy, you think, "How can I, a holy, righteous, perfect person give room to that temptation? That's not who I am. I have been delivered from sin. I am the spitting image of God, created in His likeness, created to glorify Him, to be intimate with Him, and not for sin. Christ lives in me. Holy Spirit lives in me. He is grieved and His voice quenched by sin. I don't want to grieve someone that I love so deeply."

Okay, now what happens if, for whatever reason, you do

Chapter 4: Grace and Sin

sin? You are still righteous. *Righteousness is the state of right relationship with God.* Righteousness is not right *doing*. It is right *being*. What you do doesn't change who you are. Who you are determines what you do.

Your kids don't stop being your kids when they misbehave. They are still your kids. His blood cleanses you of all your sins. Holy Spirit convicts you of righteousness, and doesn't put you down and make you feel guilty. You thank God that your relationship with Him is still intact. You are still His child. He loves you just like He always did and you love Him in response to His overwhelming, marvelous love. Once you know who you are you realize that it was absolutely, absurdly out of character for you to sin, because that is not who you are. You are a holy, righteous, perfect person. You simply believed a lie outside of your Christ-like nature and sinned as a result of a lapse of judgment. You realize that you made a mistake by acting out of character, and you decide that going forward you will walk according to who you really are. You determine that you will be who you are—holy, righteous and perfect.

Let me give you an example of a time when Holy Spirit convicted me of righteousness. I was on a trip, preaching in India. As part of my daily exercise, I was hiking up a mountain when I saw a poor, elderly man carrying an unwieldy forty-lb. bag up the mountain. I asked my guide about him and he said that he made his living by carrying bags of rice up the 3000-ft. mountain three times a week, to sell to the people at the top. As a result of carrying such heavy loads his back was permanently bent. At that time I was stirred to give him money, but I didn't. Later, Holy Spirit convicted me, saying that I should have given him money. Now, because I knew that Holy Spirit wasn't convicting me of sin, I didn't feel any guilt or condemnation. Nor did I feel regret that I had missed my chance. Instead, I thanked Him for convicting me of righteousness (of who I am, and of the right thing to do) and decided that the next time I saw the poor old man, I would bless him with money. Two days later, as I was coming down the mountain, the same man was going up, and that time I was able to bless him with money when our paths crossed. This is how the Holy Spirit convicts us of righteousness. He doesn't convict believers of sinfulness, as we don't have the sin nature anymore, because Jesus has delivered us of our old sin nature.

You are Like God

The words 'likeness' and 'fellowship' have the same Greek root. You are like God only when you are in fellowship with Him, when you realize that you have been crucified with Christ and that you no longer live, but Christ lives in you. Some of us know it. Others don't. It is our responsibility to share the gospel with those who don't.

People who refuse to believe the truth that Jesus has died as them, and that they are in Christ, won't benefit from this truth, either in this life or the next. There is a hell for those who won't receive God's love for them. However, God doesn't send anyone to hell. It is each person's personal choice. But it is a shame that some of those who have been set free from hell still choose to go there. That is where we come in. Our mission is to share God's love and His 'almost too good to be true' gospel with everyone. God wants everyone to be with Him both in this life and forever.

Chapter 5: Grace, not Works

Romans 11:6 says "And if by grace, then it is no longer of works; otherwise grace is no longer grace. But if it is of works, it is no longer grace; otherwise work is no longer work".

So which gospel are we preaching? Are we really preaching Paul's gospel? The main problem is that many are uncomfortable apart from a combination of grace and works. However, the two just don't mix. You can either have works or you can have grace, but you cannot have both.

1 Kings 18:21 asks, "How long will you falter between two opinions?" Then James 1:8 goes on to state that, "A double-minded man is unstable in all his ways."

But Paul says clearly in Romans 11:6 that we cannot have a mixture of grace and works. A grace-works mixture or conditional grace is an oxymoron and an impossibility that completely undermines the definition of grace. *Grace is unconditional.* In fact, Paul devotes most of the Book of Romans to proving that by works of the law we cannot attain the righteousness of God.

Romans 10:3-4 says, "For they being ignorant of God's righteousness, and seeking to establish their own righteousness, have not submitted to the righteousness of God. For Christ is the end of the law for righteousness to everyone who believes".

The Do-Get Paradigm

Many people believe that only a person who practices religious traditions like circumcision and animal sacrifices is trusting in the law for his salvation. However, the reality is that if your motive for doing something is to deserve and earn God's blessings or to please God, you are in the law paradigm. Grace is what God gives us freely, and is not based on what we do, but rather it is based on His desire to give solely because of His great love for us and the finished work of Christ. If you are still in the do-get/do-to-be paradigm (I do in order to get/do in order to be or please), then you are trying to earn God's favor by your good deeds and are still living by works.

By its very definition God's grace cannot be earned, and is freely given. If I give you something free with no strings attached, what do you have to do to earn it? The answer is nothing, nada, zip! You cannot earn something that is free. Most believers aren't walking in the blessings of God because they are trying to earn something that can only be received freely. The key to walking in God's blessings is to understand, recognize and realize what He has already given you and live in them, knowing that they are yours. This principle applies equally to walking full of His anointing.

Most of us don't have a problem believing that we're forgiven of our sins and so we tend to walk in that reality. However, it's worth noting: the same verse in Isaiah that says that He was bruised for our iniquities, also says we are healed by His stripes. And if that's the case, then why do we find it difficult to believe we're healed? Quite often it is because we believe that God either causes or allows sickness and disease as a form of discipline or to purify our character. This belief is the result of not rightly discerning the body of Christ[1]. Many of us are sick, not because of God's judgment but because we just don't believe Isaiah 53:5 that says: "By His stripes we are healed." Instead we attribute to God, atrocities that none of us would ever dream of inflicting on our own children, and in so doing we've made God out to be a child abuser of the worst sort. Would you stand by and willingly allow someone to abuse your kids?

If we believe that God gave us the sickness, or that He's

allowing our marriage to fall apart just to teach us something, then we would have to believe this was God's will; and if it was God' will we would want to do everything we could to remain in this condition and stay in God's will. We wouldn't have the faith for healing, or for our marriage to be restored.

The fact is that God is good. Just as we deeply cherish our own children, God only wants the very best for us—to protect and provide for us, and to give us good health. He has freely provided all these things for us because of His deep and abiding love. These blessings cannot be received by doing something to please Him or earn His favor. We just need to thank Him and walk in the river of continuous blessings in expectation of His goodness.

I Am vs. I Am Not

In our traditional mindset, we have been trained in an 'I am not' theology instead of an 'I am' theology. We have been trained to think that 'we are not' and therefore we need to make up for our inadequacy by doing all kinds of works to gradually improve who we are. We think, "I'm not good enough, holy enough or righteous enough." As a result, we are unhappy; we are not healed, and we have neither joy nor peace. Instead of living the abundant life, we are unfulfilled, and disappointed. We have no confidence in ourselves, or in our day-to-day relationships at work or at home. We have poor self-esteem, and a terrible self-image. So we are sick, lacking, and feel guilty most of the time, filled with shame and fear of anything and everything. We have succeeded in creating a worldwide Christian community that is living an unnatural, guilt-driven lifestyle. This was not God's intent for us when He created us. We look for ways to feel bad about ourselves and wallow in self-pity about how worthless we are.

We are always trying to become something that we can never be. So we are always short and lacking. Religion always keeps us short of something we can never be.

God tells Moses in Exodus 3:14: "I AM WHO I AM." God's name is I AM. Jesus came to earth as the I AM. He said, "I am the way, the truth and the life. I am the Resurrection and the Life. I am the Bread of life. I am the Light of life," and much more. You've been created in the image of the living God. He has united himself with you[2] and grafted you into Himself[3]. You are now one with I AM, who lives in you and through you. You are holy, righteous, perfect, pure and innocent. You are healed by His stripes[4]. You don't have a spirit of fear, but of love, power and a sound mind[5]. You have the love of God in you[6], and all your needs are always met in Christ Jesus[7]. You can do all things through Christ who strengthens you[8]. You have joy unspeakable and full of glory[9] and the peace that passes understanding[10]. He is 'I AM'—all that you need whenever you need it, and He is living in you and is one with you. Let us walk in the fullness of His abundant, overflowing life.

The gospel is a coming of age message. The language of Ephesians 1 is a Bar mitzvah message. Before you had this revelation, you were like a boy without identity and privileges. So you lived below your privileges of adulthood. You lived in ignorance. Now you realize that you are a man. You are now an adult. Religion has kept us below our privileges for life, because we could never become anything of value. As an adult, you now realize that you are holy. So you don't have any excuse for not being holy. You are now complete. So you don't live with a constant feeling of inadequacy and incompleteness. You are now whole. You don't have to always have a feeling of emptiness and sadness. You have now reached a state of permanent fullness, completeness and wholeness. You can always be happy, complete and full. No more sadness, no more fear, no more inadequacy, no more feeling that you are not good enough.

I love this simple song that Francois Du Toit sings. "He is I am in me. He is I am in you. He is I am in mankind. In Him we are reconciled."

Salvation Isn't Just Spiritual

Ephesians 2:8 clearly says, "For by grace you have been saved through faith, and that not of yourselves; it is the gift of God."

This isn't just referring to salvation in the spiritual sense. The word for saved/salvation, *sozo*, actually means much, much more. It means *saved, healed, delivered, set free, restored, complete, made whole, blessed and prospered*. This principle of Ephesians 2:8 applies to every aspect of our lives. Our healing is by grace. Our provision is by grace. We are under God's protection every time we leave the house. We have all these things by grace: it is not something we obtain because of what we do. These things don't happen because we're good people, but because of the incredible love of our heavenly Father—because of His abundant grace!

We obviously have a part to play in salvation. We need to enter into our relationship with the Triune God by partaking of the New Covenant in Christ. As we start knowing Him more through His word and through fellowship with Him, we can enter more and more into the fullness of all that He has for us. We will start enjoying His love, peace and joy. We can experience deliverance from bondages and addictions. We can live in freedom, health and abundant life that the Lord has designed for us.

Recently I overheard a phone conversation my wife had with her sister. They were excitedly exclaiming how blessed they were in every way. Folks, these principles really work! You may say, "I tried it, but I still have many daunting issues in my life." Living by grace and not by works requires a change in our way of thinking and lifestyle. It doesn't come overnight in a brief trial run. It doesn't come by trying. It comes by understanding who we are and changing our vision to see ourselves as God sees us.

So how can we make this a reality?

The Perfect Law of Liberty

James 1:22-25 says: "But be doers of the word, and not hearers only, deceiving yourselves. For if anyone is a hearer of the word and not a doer, he is like a man observing his natural face in a mirror; for he observes himself, goes away, and immediately forgets what kind of man he was. But he who looks into the perfect law of liberty and continues in it, and is not a forgetful hearer but a doer of the work, this one will be blessed in what he does."

Verse 22 is a favorite verse for 'works proponents' to say that we must be *doers* of the Word. I love Francois Du Toit's interpretation of verse 22[11]. The Word 'doers' is the Greek word *poietes* from which we get the word poetry. This verse isn't telling us to follow the law, or its enhanced version that we presume is in the New Testament. This verse is saying, *"Continue to look into this mirror until what you see makes poetry out of your life."* Poetry is a spontaneous, natural outflow of a heart bubbling with excitement and joy.

In other words—look into this perfect law of liberty and keep on looking until what you see becomes a spontaneous, joyful response that can't be contained, flowing out of your very being! God has created you with total freedom. He just wants you to be yourself and have a blast being who you are!

When you look in the mirror, you see who you truly

Chapter 5: Grace, not Works

are. According to the mirror of God's Word, you are a holy, righteous, perfect person, created in the image of God, exactly like Jesus. Now, you could take a quick glance at yourself, then leave and forget what you saw. That is the person that James is referring to in verse 24, "for he observes himself, goes away, and immediately forgets what kind of man he was." You can slip right back into your old ways of life and into your old addictions.

Or, you can be like the man in James 1:25 where we read, "But he who looks into the perfect law of liberty and continues in it, and is not a forgetful hearer but a doer of the work, this one will be blessed in what he does."

This is how you start to live in your true identity. James 1:22-24 is clearly a passage on identity, but our law mentality has made it a passage on works.

You could make a concerted determination that you will look into the mirror of the Word and keep on looking until what you see there spontaneously flows out of your very core and becomes like your second nature, and is actually your true nature. The Word reflects your true nature—who you really are. God just wants you to see who you are and be yourself! He isn't trying to change you and make you into something else. He created you uniquely in His image to be yourself! This is the message of the New Covenant.

Hebrews 8:10-13 tells us, "For this is the covenant that I will make with the house of Israel after those days, says the Lord: I will put My laws in their mind and write them on their hearts; and I will be their God, and they shall be My people. None of them shall teach his neighbor, and none his brother, saying, 'Know the Lord,' for all shall know Me, from the least of them to the greatest of them. For I will be merciful to their unrighteousness, and their sins and their lawless deeds I will remember no more. In that He says, 'A new covenant', He has made the first covenant obsolete. Now what is becoming obsolete and growing old is ready to vanish away."

The Law was Never God's Plan for Us

God never intended for us to live by a set of laws. The law was an interim arrangement to prevent man from his downward spiral of sin into destruction. The law was God's temporary arrangement for man until Jesus came and gave us the New Covenant of Hebrews 8:10-13. Since the life, death, resurrection and ascension of Jesus, we are united with Him and have a heart of flesh. We now have His laws downloaded into our minds and hearts, so that we have become a dynamic model of righteousness, where we are living epistles—breathing, talking and walking reflections of Jesus.

Dr. Myles Munroe says this[12] "God never intended to write down any of His laws for us. He did not want us to have to read in order to live. There was no written law in the Garden of Eden, no written law for Abraham, no written law at all for God's covenant people until the days of Moses. The King of Heaven's intention was to write His laws on our hearts and minds so that we needed no other teacher. The law was only necessary due to humanity's rebellion and separation from God. We needed something to restrain our baser nature and instincts and prevent us from destroying ourselves by uncontrolled selfishness, passions, and violence. The King's goal has never changed. Despite mankind's rebellion, His original purpose still stands."

This unchanging purpose of the King was fulfilled in the New Covenant through Jesus Christ.

Once man fell, instead of living in close relationship with God, he began to live out of his own selfish will and increasingly evil imaginations. He drifted further and further away from the life God designed for him. Over time man became corrupt and out of control—in an endless downward spiral toward destruction. God introduced the law to man to call a halt to this desperate cycle. This was a stopgap measure till the fullness of time came, when our Savior Jesus would come to deliver and rescue us. Galatians 3:24 says: "Therefore the **law was our tutor** *to bring us* to Christ, that we might be justified by faith."

Notice that the phrase *to bring us* is in italics, denoting that this wasn't in the original Greek language and was added by translators. This verse actually reads: "The law was our tutor till Christ, that we might be justified by faith."

Behold and Be Who You Are

Now let's look at 2 Corinthians 3:18 (Amplified): "And all of us, as with unveiled face, [because we] continued to behold [in the Word of God] as in a mirror the glory of the Lord, are constantly being transfigured into His very own image in ever-increasing splendor and from one degree of glory to another; [for this comes] from the Lord [Who is] the Spirit."

This is the model for our Christian walk. We keep looking into the mirror at who we are. We are in the image of Jesus, the perfect man. Ephesians 4:13 says: "Till we all come to the unity of the faith and of the knowledge of the Son of God, to a perfect man, to the measure of the stature of the fullness of Christ." Jesus is the perfect man, and we have already been filled to overflowing with His fullness.

Colossians 2:9-10 says: "For in Him dwells all the fullness of the Godhead bodily; and you are complete in Him, who is the head of all principality and power." This verse says that the fullness of the Godhead dwells in Christ. The word 'complete' in verse 10 is the same word as 'fullness' in verse 9, but it is in the Greek perfect tense, meaning that you have the same fullness of Christ on a continuous, ongoing basis.

Now, let's take a closer look at what this means. What do you see when you look in a mirror? You see yourself. You don't see what you could potentially be. When you look into the mirror, you see your true self. And this verse says that our true self is in the image of the Son of God, a perfect man. You look at your perfect self that is filled with the fullness of God. Then as you continue to look there is a natural outflow of the expression of the fullness of God from your inner being. You are transformed from glory to glory. You are transformed from the glory of your natural self into the glory of the fullness of the Spirit of God.

You may think that God has a little bit of His fullness in you, a little in me and a little bit of His fullness in everyone else. No! We each have all of His fullness inside us. Our technology has advanced to a level where it is now possible to store a whole library on a little USB stick. The contents of a USB stick can be simultaneously copied to multiple computers/devices. How much more would God's technology, that is far superior to any human technology that we could ever have, be able to fill every person in the world with the entire fullness of God? As you see yourself for who you really are, in the image of God, filled with all the fullness of God, out of your belly will flow rivers of His glory wherever you go[13]. Rivers of His love, rivers of His peace, rivers of His joy will flood everyone you meet, as you go about your daily activities.

As you look at yourself in the mirror of God, repentance takes place. The word that is translated 'repentance' is the Greek word *metanoia*. The English word 'repentance' came out of Augustinian beliefs that mistakenly associated *metanoia* with penance. However, the Greek word *metanoia* makes no reference to penance of any kind. In other words, there is absolutely no

Chapter 5: Grace, not Works

need for any grief, lamentation, weeping or rending your heart or garments. *Metanoia* simply means a change of mind—to continuously change the way you think—and it happens on an ongoing basis. *Metanoia* is taking place in you as you read this book.

As you continue to look in the mirror and see who you really are, your mindsets keep changing. This process isn't limited to once a week at church. He created us for continuous, intimate fellowship with Him. He continuously speaks to us, and we can respond to Him in the same way.

In Matthew 4:4, Jesus said: "Man shall not live by bread alone, but by every word that proceeds from the mouth of God." Clearly, we can have intimate ongoing conversations with Him as we go about our normal daily activities. Metanoia can take place throughout the week as He speaks to us and we see ourselves for who we really are.

Let's take a sneak peek into the second half of this book on your identity, as it relates to this discussion. Your true identity isn't in Adam. On the contrary, you were created in the image of the Son of God. Adam walked with God in the cool of the day. God was outside of Adam, but now that you are in Christ, God indwells you in the Person of the Holy Spirit. You are in union with Christ[2] who actually lives in you[14].

There are two parts to your identity: (1) You were created in His image for the purpose of fellowship and intimacy with God and (2) You were created in His image so that He could come and live in you and you could enjoy this world and the people around you together with God.

As you keep focusing on who you really are, you are continually being transformed into the image that you see, from glory to glory into the image of God. The key is to keep looking and not lose sight of who you are.

Faith is by Grace. Faith is Not a Work

Ephesians 2:8 says, "For by grace you have been saved through faith, and that not of yourselves; it is the gift of God."

Faith is quite often interpreted as something we do. We have been taught to think that faith means to confess, decree or declare what we desire until we have it. But Ephesians 2:8 says that it is the gift of God. It is not your faith. It is the faith of God. Have you ever been told that you were sick because of your lack of faith? Sometimes we believe that if something bad happens to us, it's because our faith is weak. But the truth is that faith isn't something we can conjure up on our own. It is not our faith to begin with; it is His faith[15]: Everything that we will ever receive from God is through the faith *of* God, in what He did for us through His original purpose and in His Incarnation. All we need to do is understand and realize that He has already given us everything that we could ever possibly need. Then we just need to enter His rest: enter into, walk in, and live in all that He has already provided for us. This scenario is much like children living with their parents. Everything that their parents have belongs to the children and the children know, realize and live accordingly. They know that they will get what they need when they need it. My two-year-old granddaughter, Selah thinks that everything and everyone in the house exist for her. She knows that she belongs—that she is one of us. Jesus told us to become like little children. He is I AM living in you, taking care of you and providing for you in all your ways.

Christ in You, the Hope of Glory

Hebrews 1:3 and John 1:14 say that Jesus was the final Word. He is God's plan. You no longer need to wonder about God's plan for your life. Your life is His plan. Christ in you, the hope of glory is His plan for your life[14]. You were created for greatness. His plan is for you to uniquely create history by just being yourself. The Apostle Paul said we are living epistles. God did everything by Himself with no help from us.

The works theology is really telling us that Jesus came and died on the cross for you, but what He did wasn't enough; We are incorrectly taught that He did a half-baked job. We have been misguided to think that we need to supplement what Jesus did by our works and that we need to pray and fast all our life to please Him or obtain any of His blessings or His anointing. We incorrectly think that we need to improve our holiness little by little throughout our life by our own efforts. We have been misled to think that God will help us only if we pray and fast. When I first started listening to grace messages a few years back, I liked and accepted most of them. But whenever someone said that I didn't need to worship, fast or pray to please God or get His blessings and His anointing, I silently disagreed with them, because my charismatic training was rooted in worshipping, fasting and praying to please God and obtain His blessings and His anointing. It took reading dozens books and listening to more than a hundred messages several times over to change my mindset, to line up with the truth about God's grace being a free gift. We pray because of our intense love for Him and because we long and yearn to constantly fellowship with Him. Prayer is a lifestyle.

The Finished Work of Christ

All it takes to walk in His salvation, His anointing and His blessings is to realize, understand and enter into His rest, into His finished work.

Okay, what is the finished work of Christ?

In John 19:30, Jesus said, "It is finished! And bowing His

head, He gave up His spirit."

The Old Covenant was finished. The system of law had served its purpose and ended. Everything that separated man and God was removed. Jesus' mission on earth, to take humanity's fallen nature on Himself and die, was also finished. The entire old creation died with Jesus. When Jesus rose from the dead, an entirely new creation came into being.

The popular version of the New Testament that we have often heard preached is that Jesus came to give us a stricter set of rules to follow. For instance, in the Old Testament, you couldn't commit adultery. Now, you can't even look at a woman to lust after her. In the Old Testament, you couldn't murder. Now, you can't even be angry with someone. The truth is that no one who has ever lived kept all the law, all the time, all their life—ever. But God knew that going in. Jesus was getting to the root of the matter in His teachings. He was dealing with heart issues. In His teachings He communicated to us the heart of what God really desired, fully aware that no man could possibly keep all of God's commandments.

Was Jesus a Grace Teacher?

No, Jesus actually preached the law on steroids. The New Covenant didn't start with Matthew. The New Covenant began after the crucifixion and resurrection of Christ.

Yes, it is true that you shouldn't look at a woman to lust after her in your heart. This is what God really desires for you. But it is not possible for you to keep all God's commandments by your own strength or efforts. That is why Jesus came and fulfilled all the law all the time, all His life on behalf of us, as us.

Andre Rabe says: "Jesus isn't an example *for* us. He is an example *of* us." We are not *merely* followers *of* Jesus; we are one

Chapter 5: Grace, not Works

with Jesus. (Emphasis mine).

Galatians 2:20 and Colossians 1:27 tell us that Christ is *in us* and that we live in union *with* Him. Jesus fulfilled *all* the law on our behalf. In the Old Testament, we were ineligible for any of God's blessings unless we obeyed all His commandments. Jesus obeyed all the commandments on our behalf, thereby making us eligible for *all* of God's blessings. He took our sin nature upon Himself and died in our place. When He rose from the dead, a new creation came into being. This new creation is in the image of Jesus, the perfect man, the original prototype of man[17].

The harsh truth is that man, by his own efforts, is completely incapable of obeying all of God's commandments. But *in union* with God, man *can* obey God's commandments, if he relies on the power and the abilities of God. Man, with God living inside of him can be obedient to God, not by his own efforts, but by the grace of God with the faith of God. If he fails to obey God at any time, he is forgiven of his sins and he can start afresh and continue to obey God with the strength given to him by God. This is possible by means of the constant communion and fellowship that he has with God, who is with him always[16].

The purpose of creation is fellowship and intimacy with God as well as fellowship with our fellow-human beings. We obey God not because we have to in order to gain His approval or to please Him. We obey Him because of our intimate relationship with Him. We love Him because He first loved us.

Much of the grace controversy is based on the fear that people would not obey God if they believed they were forgiven in advance. But let's examine that belief in the light of what we've learned. We obey God because of our close relationship of love with Him. When we get a revelation of His love for us and our relationship with Him, sin loses its appeal.

How Does God See You?

The traditional motivation for prayer and intercession is to persuade a reluctant God to bless and deliver a sinful people. But the truth is that we don't pray in order to please God or to get something from Him. We pray because of our close relationship with Him and because we want to be with Him. He is already pleased with us because of His eternal purpose and because Jesus has completely restored *our* eternal purpose.

Nor do we read the Word to please Him. We read the Word in order to hear His voice because of our love relationship with Him. God is deeply enamored of you.

Song of Solomon 4:9 says: "You have ravished my heart with one look of your eyes."

He intricately designed you for intimacy with Him before the foundation of the world. He has been dreaming about you from eternity. From the moment you were born, He has set His eyes on you and has been watching over you. He has protected you and provided for you all through your life.

No one has ever loved you the way He does. In His eyes, you are the most beautiful person on earth[18]. He sees you as perfect. He says in Isaiah 1:18: "Though your sins are like scarlet, they shall be as white as snow; though they are red like crimson, they shall be as wool." To God, you are as white as snow; you are as pure as the whitest wool!

Song of Solomon 4:7 tells us: "You are all fair, my love, and there is no spot in you." You are spotless! Another translation says, "You are flawless." You are like a flawless diamond with no inclusions! Some of you are thinking, "Well, I wouldn't go that far." You probably think I'm exaggerating the love of God, but I'm telling it like it is. Any exaggeration of His love would be an understatement of the true extent of His love for you.

In many places where I've preached, I've asked this question, "How many of you think your child is the most beautiful child on earth?" Then I asked for a show of hands. In every place, everyone who had children raised their hands to say that they thought that their child was the most beautiful person on earth. That shouldn't come as any surprise. You are a child of God. In exactly the same way that we delight in our beautiful children, He thinks you are the most beautiful person on earth.

Then I asked those who had two or more children if they loved one child more than another. Unanimously, all parents who had children raised their hands to say that they loved all their children equally. In the same way, God loves all His children equally. And if that's true, I think it would be fair to say that He loves you most in the world, because He doesn't love anyone more than He loves you.

Song of Solomon 6:5 says, "Turn your eyes away from me, for they have overcome me." He is captivated by just one look of your eyes. He is overcome with one glance from you. That being the case, it would be impossible to even imagine that He would bring sickness, accidents and trouble on you. God is never the cause of evil, but He does turn evil around for your good.

God is Better than Good

The love and goodness of God cannot be exaggerated. However good you may imagine God to be, His goodness is far more than that. However much you think God loves you, He loves you more than that.

About fifteen years ago, I was a prayer leader of ANHOP (All Nations House of Prayer), in Grand Prairie, Texas, two hours a day, six days a week for three years. After that, I was prayer leader in RCHOP (River City House of Prayer), in San Antonio, Texas for about three years. Quite often, we would dwell on the goodness of God. I would say, "God is good." Then I would add, "He is better than good. He is better than better than good." Then I would finally say, "He is better than better than better than better than…good!" He far exceeds your wildest understanding of His goodness. In fact, when you contemplate His goodness, when you meditate on how much He loves you, the last thing on your mind is sin or disobedience.

Jesus said in John 14:15, "If you love me, you will obey my commandments." Jesus isn't saying that you need to prove you love Him by obeying His commandments, as is most commonly taught. When you are captivated by His love, obedience is the natural outcome. Obedience is a natural outflow of love. Sadly, in our churches we have made it drudgery—an obligation. We say, "If you want God to bless you, you must obey Him. You must obey Him in order to please Him." We need to get out of our Do-Get or Do-to-be/please mindset and shift to a mindset where we bask in His amazing love and acceptance.

God Isn't Mad at You

Jesus says in Matthew 5:17: "I came not to destroy, but to fulfill the law," and He did just that in the Incarnation.

Matthew 11:13 says that the law and the prophets were until John. In other words we are no longer living under a law-based covenant. That Old Covenant lasted only until John the Baptist.

The cross ushered in an entirely new era, an entirely new

way of thinking. Isaiah 54:10 says this: "I am going to establish with you a covenant of loving kindness." God said He was going to establish with us a covenant that is based on love. This was God's plan from the very beginning.

Hebrews 8:10-12 defines the New Covenant in which we currently live. In Isaiah 54:9 God says this about our sins: "For this is like the waters of Noah to Me; For as I have sworn that the waters of Noah would no longer cover the earth, so have I sworn that I would not be angry with you, nor rebuke you."

God promised Noah that He would never flood the entire earth again, and He has kept that promise. In Isaiah 54:9 He swears that He will never be angry with you again nor will He rebuke you.

Even if God didn't swear, His Word would be truer than anything anyone could say. But God is swearing—making a vow that He cannot break. Do you know why? Because He knew that there would be millions of Christians spreading lies that our God is an angry God who would send people who didn't believe in Him, to hell. Jesus did not preach a 'Turn or Burn' gospel. In Isaiah 54:9 we see that just as He has kept His promise that He would never flood the earth again, He will keep His promise that He won't be angry with you. Here it is, in plain English, right in the middle of the Bible. How much clearer could He be? Yet we hear the widespread message of grace mixed with works that portrays Him as an angry judgmental God.

We hear televangelists, famous preachers and prophets prophesying against places like New Orleans, stating that God's judgment will come against New Orleans because of some of the sinful aspects of Mardi Gras that take place every year. When Hurricane Katrina hit New Orleans, they said that this was God's judgment on New Orleans. Well, if it was, then God sure was a poor shot, because He missed Bourbon Street completely, leaving it untouched. That is the street on which some of the sinful aspects of Mardi Gras celebration take place every year.

We have prophets gone wild, prophesying the big one (an 8.0 earthquake) on California. Others say the 9/11 bombings were God's judgment on America. They say that the tsunami in Asia was God's judgment on the heathen. We are portraying the Christian God as a judgmental God. We think God only loves those who believe in Him and that God is angry with people of other religions who worship idols. So when a tsunami hits Indonesia, we declare that God is judging them because they are people of a different religion who don't believe in God. The fact is that God loves them more than any of us have ever loved our children. Acts 17: 28 says, "For in Him we live and move and have our being, as also some of your own poets have said, 'For we are also His offspring.'"

'We live and move and have our being in Him' isn't just a worship song. It's in the Bible. Paul spoke this to idol-worshiping Athenians, telling them that they were His offspring. God so loved His offspring (the world) that He gave His only begotten Son that whoever believes in Him should not perish[12].

Let's just think about this mindset. If we think that God is angry with those who believe in other gods and prophesy judgment and destruction on them, how can we love them enough to lead them to Christ? We couldn't, because we believe that judgment is God's will for them. We think it is God's will to destroy them. And then, when the tsunami strikes them, we inwardly gloat that they got what they deserved, though we may not say that out loud, in order to be politically correct. Let me ask you a question: Was that the mindset of Jesus? Absolutely not! Jesus said: "I did not come to judge the world, but to save the world." The Word also says in John 3:16: "For God so loved the world that He gave His only begotten Son, that whoever believes in Him should not perish." Somewhere along the road, we have completely missed it. We are not living like Jesus lived, or preaching the gospel that Jesus or Paul preached. If anything, we have adopted an opposing position. Christianity is perceived by many as one of the most intolerant religions in the world because of this mindset. This in itself is a huge deterrent to people coming to Jesus.

Now, let's look at the mindset of the true gospel of Jesus Christ. God is madly in love with everyone in New Orleans, whether saint or sinner. God is crazy about the beautiful Moslems of Indonesia, whether they know Jesus or not. God is not angry with them. The Father loves them so much that He sent Jesus to die for them. He has given to us the message of reconciliation. The message that we are to preach to them is that God loves them so much that Jesus died for them and that their sins are forgiven. All they need to do is come to a saving knowledge of Jesus Christ.

No More Law

In Romans 10:4 we read that Christ is the end of law to all who believe.

The New Covenant isn't a law-based covenant. It is a grace-based covenant.

Galatians 3:24 says the law was our tutor to bring us to Christ.

Grace is not a license to sin. It is the key to overcoming sin.

Romans 6:15 (Mirror Bible)[25] says: "Being under grace and not under the law most certainly does not mean that you now have a license to sin."

Most of the body of Christ is still on a never-ending

treadmill of works—on an endless cycle of works, guilt and repentance when they fail. The Christian life is a roller coaster for many people. They know that the Bible asks us to be happy. But how can you be happy if you are in a shame-guilt-repentance cycle most of your life? This is due to the prevalent teaching in the body of Christ that you have *to do* to be: you must do things to be pleasing to God. So the Christian life is usually a constant attempt to please a God who could get angry with you and punish you at the slightest provocation. This is law-based living out of religious obligation. However, in the paradigm of grace, we are motivated by our close and loving relationship with Jesus.

Then there are the over-achievers who want to be really pleasing to God, and think they have to pray several hours a day, fast for days on end and go and preach the gospel in order to be pleasing to God. We pray and preach the gospel because that is what we want to do, and not in order to gain God's approval. Our God isn't an angry God[20]. He's a loving, merciful, happy God.

You Don't Have the Sin Nature

There is another deception that is the bane of the church. We think that we still have the sin nature. We have a dualistic mindset that makes us think we have a spiritual side and a fleshly side. We think we must overcome our flesh on a day-to-day basis and that we become holier and holier with time. This mindset believes that maybe after forty years of walking with Jesus, we will be 80% holy and far more pleasing to God than we once were, but we will still only be truly pleasing to God when we die and go to heaven. As a result of these and other similar teachings, we think that the objective of our life is to become purer and holier and everything else is secondary. We think that God has put us on earth to test how good we can be so that one day, when we get to heaven, He can reward us accordingly.

So we have all this hue and cry about grace from all the folks with that particular mindset. They think we're corrupting churchgoers who they have unsuccessfully been trying to motivate all these years to do more, more, and more—to please God, purely from the perspective of a heavenly reward. They think that if people believe the grace message, they'll stop doing the few church activities they're doing now.

God Created us to Enjoy Life

God created us to enjoy life now.

Jesus tells us in John 10:10 "I have come that they may have life, and that they may have *it* more abundantly. "

1 Timothy 6:17 says that God gave us richly all things to enjoy.

God didn't create us to live a miserable life of denial for the sole purpose of working our way to heaven. God created us to live life to its fullest in union with Christ in the here and now. Of course, we will go to heaven someday. But He created the earth to be so beautiful for us to enjoy life with Him and our fellow-human beings.

The fact is that God is already pleased with you because of what Jesus has done. Ephesians 1:6 says that you are accepted in the beloved.

Luke 3:22 says "This is my beloved son in whom I am well pleased."

That makes you His beloved son/daughter in whom He is well pleased.

What Jesus did, you did. When He died, you died. Jesus came and lived on this earth as you, was baptized as you and died as you. When He rose again, you came forth as a new creation, re-created in His image. When He ascended on high, you ascended with Him and are now seated with Him in the heavenlies[21].

2 Corinthians 5:21 says He made you righteous. You're no longer a sinner; you are a saint. When Paul wrote his letters to the saints at Ephesus and Corinthians, he was addressing all of them, not just a few of the Ephesians and Corinthians who were saints.

The issue with the fall was taken care of in the Incarnation of Jesus. Sin separated man from God, who, in His immense wisdom, took care of the sin problem and made you holy, righteous and perfect—one with the Holy Spirit, who lives inside you. He made you all that He wanted you to be. Now, you just need to recognize this truth and walk in your new identity.

Why is it so difficult for people to believe that God has made us holy, righteous and perfect? Is it because we think it's impossible for God? God intricately designed and created the earth, sun, moon, stars, the beautiful birds, animals and sea creatures, and eventually created human beings in perfection. Just the anatomy of a human being is so mind-boggling that it should convince us that nothing is impossible with God. If He could do all that, why is it hard to believe that He took care of the sin problem and made us perfect?

Why is it hard to believe that the Omnipotent God made you holy, righteous and perfect? If you or I were God, we may have had Jesus come and do a halfway job of taking care of our sin problem, and let man work through the rest of his issues for as long as he lived. But we have been set free from the law of sin and death! Romans 8:2 says: "For the law of the Spirit of life in

Christ Jesus has made me free from the law of sin and death."

No More Distance, No More Delay

Our traditional teachings specialize in distance and delay. We have been taught that God is someone far away, high and lifted up who can't look upon us because of our sins. This couldn't be further from the truth. Throughout the ages, God has been going after His people and wooing them back to Him. His plan from the foundation of the world was to be close to us. Jesus came to earth as a true representation of the Father.

Hebrews 1:3 says this on the subject: "being the brightness of *His* glory and the express image of His person."

Jesus came to earth to reveal the heart of the Father.

In John 14:9 He said: "He who has seen me has seen the Father."

In his book, *Welcome Home—Opening the Door to the Nature of God,* Author Mike Miller said this: "This scripture calls upon us to interpret the Father through the biblical revelation of Jesus. There's no other way presented as an alternative. We are to interpret the Father by the Son, not by our experiences in a fallen world; not through apathetic, complacent religious doctrines; not through the lens of the Law. We're to base our interpretation of the Father on the revelation of Jesus Christ alone."[27]

Quite often we are taught that the Father is angry and Jesus came to appease His anger. We tend to think that we don't want to be left alone in the room with the Father without Jesus. But the Father never left Jesus, not even while He was on the cross.

God is Closer Than the Air You Breathe

Paul says in Ephesians 5:31: ". . . and be joined to his wife, and the two shall become one flesh." This is talking about the closeness God designed for a husband and wife. But God is closer to you than a man is to his wife.

We read in 1 Corinthians 6:17: "But he who is joined to the Lord is one spirit with Him."

According to Galatians 2:20 we are united—one with Christ. We are one spirit with Him. A man and his wife become one flesh, but we as believers are one spirit with the Lord. God wanted to be so close to us that when Jesus died, we died and when He rose from the dead, we rose as new creations, united with Him. Now He is in us[22], with us[23] and for us[24] in everything we do. He is closer to you than the air you breathe. He knows the very number of hairs on your head; He knows your next word before you speak it. His name says it all: *Immanuel*, which means God with us.

Here and Now

The performance mode then pushes almost every blessing of God either to heaven or to the millennium after the Rapture. Whether we believe it or not God didn't create us and put us here on earth to be miserable, as a test, to grade us for our life in heaven. Why would God create our beautiful earth and put us here if His goal for us was limited to being pleased with us in heaven? He could have saved himself the trouble and simply created us in heaven, but He didn't do that. He planned every intricate aspect of each of our personalities before the foundation of the earth and created the earth for us to enjoy.

True Freedom in Christ

Because of the dual-nature mindset and the belief that our spirit is saved while our soul and body are not, the church

Chapter 5: Grace, not Works

has set its focus solely on getting holy enough to get to heaven, and getting others to heaven. Instead, if we believe in the finished work of Jesus and can get a better understanding of why we are here on earth, we'll be able to enjoy ourselves here in God's company and be happy every day of our lives. Come on—get a life!

Some of you are thinking, *well, what about this scripture, or that scripture?* The truth is that we need to understand every scripture in light of the finished work of Christ. Our understanding will be clear when we look through the lens of the finished work of Christ. When we look through the clouded lens of works, these things make no sense whatever.

When I came to the U.S. in 1990, I went to get my driver's license. I had driven in India for eighteen years before that. In India, driving is chaotic and even dangerous. My sister-in-law, who had never driven in India, went with me to the testing site to take her test. She passed and I failed. And after that I failed three more times because I had to unlearn my chaotic pattern of driving in India and re-learn the orderly way of driving required in the U.S.

In the same way, most of us have had our vision clouded by an Old Testament understanding of the Scriptures. It will take a great deal of repentance (changing the way we think) and renewing of our minds to see through the lens of the finished work of the cross. Ever since I heard about these amazing truths, I have been devouring as much material as I could: reading the books by the authors in my references section and repeatedly listening to all the messages of these wonderful men of God, to transform my thinking. I am in the process of unlearning the grace-works mixture theology that has so saturated my mind for over thirty years. I'm absolutely amazed at the freedom I've discovered through the true gospel of Jesus Christ!

So far we have discussed the traditional view of grace. Now we are going to look behind the scenes at how grace works.

Chapter 6: Are we only 1/3 Saved?

I have great news for you! You really are saved—lock, stock and barrel! You are not schizophrenic and neither is God. Nor are you a victim of a Jekyll and Hyde Syndrome. You don't have a carnal side and a spiritual side. You no longer have a sin nature.

When I used to believe I had a sin nature that I had to overcome by the Spirit, I used to want to stay 'prayed up' so that I was always in the Spirit, and not walking in the flesh. Believe it or not, a couple of years ago I read a book with a whole chapter given to how we are only 1/3 saved.

Over the past few decades most believers have sat under the teaching that originated in the early part of the last century. It teaches that man is a tri-part being composed of spirit, soul and body, but that of the three, only your spirit is saved. This teaching is based on the incorrect interpretation of Romans 7 and a few other passages of Scripture. It is true that we renew our minds daily[1] and that we present our bodies to God as a living sacrifice, but that doesn't mean our soul and body are not also saved.[3]

The body and emotions are neither good nor bad. They are amoral. They can be used either for good or bad. Our body is now the temple of the Holy Ghost[2], bought at a high price. Our bodies are now instruments of righteousness to be used for God's glory.

Because we have some incorrect foundational teachings on repentance, we have a dualistic teaching regarding almost every other aspect of our scriptural doctrine. Now, I'm not knocking the authors of these teachings. In fact, I actually believed that way for more than three decades myself. It's only by God's grace that I recently discovered the truth. I'm simply describing the deception of the teaching itself.

A Brief History of the Grace Movement

Revelation of Scripture has always been a progressive process. During the Dark Ages much of the revelation of our early church fathers was lost. Beginning with Martin Luther in the 16th Century, the progressive revelation of the Word accelerated. Typically, new revelations were ushered in by great revivals of their time, but often when the next level of revelation came, those involved in past great revivals opposed the new teaching, and simply remained content to stay in their old revelation. For example, Baptists were responsible for the discovery of the truth about being born again/saved. Later, Pentecostals and Charismatics came along with their revelation about the Holy Spirit accompanied by divine healing and speaking in tongues. Many of the Baptists held on to their teaching, but refused to be open to new revelation, and are still stuck in that place today. Many believers still don't believe divine healing is for today.

Towards the end of the last century, we had the Prophetic and Apostolic movements. Apostle Bill Hamon wrote an entire book called 'Prophets and the Prophetic Movement' that deals with the history of the various moves of God.

Consider this: During the Exodus when the cloud moved, the Israelites moved with the cloud. In the same way, members of particular moves of God were greatly blessed during the time it occurred. But those who weren't willing to move into the glory and deeper revelation when they occurred were left behind and stayed in the level of revelation that they had.

The Patriarchs of the Protestant Church

Without the progressive revelation from the various reformers in the church who came before us, we wouldn't be where we are today. Baptists built upon the revelation of Luther, Wesley, Calvin and many others. Pentecostals built upon the revelation of Baptists and all the great men and women of God before them. Charismatics then built upon the revelation of Pentecostals and all others before them.

The Heroes of the Grace Movement

More recently, we have had some amazing revelations from many great men and women of God that have been remarkably liberating. They have built upon the truths of all the preceding moves of God and received various aspects of the revelation of the Grace movement. They will all go down in history as the heroes of faith like Martin Luther, John and Charles Wesley, John Calvin, John G. Lake, E.W. Kenyon, Kenneth Hagin and many other amazing men and women of God.

Joseph Prince has amazing teachings about forgiveness and freedom from guilt and shame[8]. John Crowder has some unique teachings that we are in union with God. I have given his books to many other well-known men of God, and they responded that this is the true gospel of Jesus Christ. Karl Barth, the 20th century Swiss reformed theologian, who is often regarded as the greatest Protestant theologian of the twentieth century, has authored amazing teachings on the Incarnation. T. F. Torrance, who was Professor of Christian Dogmatics at the University of Edinburg took Karl Barth's teachings to a whole new level and hit it out of the park with his spectacular teachings on the Incarnation and the Atonement. Francois Du Toit's Mirror Bible[6] has no parallel. Andre Rabe's books and messages, offered free on his website, are amazing and life-changing. C. Baxter Kruger's books and messages are outstanding. Many of these men of God build on the teachings of Karl Barth and T.F. Torrance.

Mike Miller's website offers more than 300 free messages on various topics like judgment and entering God's rest that are second to none[9].

Jeff Turner's 'Saints in the Arms of a Happy God' is a unique, in-depth treatise that proves that God is not an angry God.

My life has been most impacted by my apostle, Ryan Pena, who offers his messages free on the Spirit and Life website. They are life changing, uncompromising, focused and clear.

Now, each of these wonderful men of God offers a different facet of the grace message. All their messages are life giving and powerful. There are also a number of other wonderful grace preachers.

The Big Picture

It is my intent in this book to bring all of them together, to show you the whole diamond in all of its glistening beauty.

If we just came out of the blue with a new teaching that didn't have some preceding foundation and basis, that teaching would be heretical. We are very thankful for all the preceding reformers who have been very instrumental in driving us in the direction of the revelation in this book. My prayer is that you would taste and see the hope and the freedom that the Lord has brought us into with these remarkable truths.

Man is Resistant to Change

As has happened in all the previous reformations, we should not be surprised to see opposition to the grace movement, because different people are wired differently, and human nature is often quite resistant to change.

A good analogy is the stock market. First there are bulls, who are very optimistic and open, eager to jump into opportunities for growth. On the other end of the spectrum are bears, who tend to see the market in a negative light. They tend to major on the risks and potential for a downturn in the market, and find it difficult to see any upside. Bears can't see opportunities for upturns in the market, and bulls can't see signs that the market is set to crash.

In the same way we find those who are so set in their ways that they are opposed to anything different from what they currently believe. Then there are those who are hungry—open to new revelation, and are willing to embrace the truths that set us free.

This is the pattern for most human beings. Most people reach a ceiling where they're willing to go with God. But He designed us to grow and keep growing—to be lifelong learners. He didn't design us to get stuck at a ceiling when it comes to revelation about Him. Thomas Merton said, "If the you of five years ago doesn't consider the you of today a heretic, you are not growing spiritually." Once the veil is lifted and you receive a new revelation, it should be difficult for you to return to where you were before. I can't believe some of the things I believed five years ago. A few years back I actually started writing a book on the Jekyll and Hyde Syndrome based on Romans 7. I had already lined up other supposedly supporting passages of scripture, like Philippians 2, Philippians 3, and Galatians 5. Thank God for His grace in delivering me from that teaching!

The Original Gospel

The authors of the articles and books with traditional teachings would make it appear that grace teachings are new truths that have burgeoned in the last decade or so. That couldn't be further from the truth. The traditional works-based dualistic teachings have their origin in Augustinian teachings from the fourth-century, so it is actually a relative newcomer. The grace message is the original Bible-based gospel that originated with the apostle Paul. Many of these truths have their roots in the teachings of church fathers like Irenaeus, John's disciple's disciple, and then from the teachings of Athanasius from the fourth century, known for his role in the Nicene creed, as well as from theologians through the 10th and 11th centuries. Karl Barth and T.F. Torrance built upon the teachings of our church fathers. Amazon offers a book by Athanasius called 'On the Incarnation'.

Is Man a Tri-Partite Being?

Now let's return to the general thinking that man is a three-part being, composed of spirit, soul and body. All through the Bible, the words 'spirit' and 'soul' are used interchangeably. Most theologians have historically held the view that man is a spiritual being, spirit/soul, living in a body/flesh. This view that the human being is comprised of spirit, soul and body originated in the early 1900s when wonderful teachers like Watchman Nee built a whole theology on 1 Thessalonians 5:23: "Now may the God of peace Himself sanctify you completely; and may your whole spirit, soul, and body be preserved blameless at the coming of our Lord Jesus Christ." They interpreted Paul's benediction to be a dissection of the human being. I read Watchman Nee's 'Spirit, Soul and Body'twice in the nineties. I have read at least a dozen of his books and bought many of them for my friends. In fact, I bought my uncle a CD collection containing fifty-three of Watchman Nee's works, and they contain some great teachings.

But dissection of the human being into three parts wasn't Paul's intention when he wrote this scripture. This was his benediction at the end of his letter to the Thessalonians telling them that their entire being should be preserved blameless. This is a 'merism'—a figure of speech like 'lock, stock and barrel.' Wikipedia defines it this way: "In law, a merism is a figure of speech by which a single thing is referred to by a conventional phrase that enumerates several of its parts, or which lists several synonyms for the same thing." The deception isn't so much in the dividing of the human being into a three-part being. The problem occurs when we use this scripture as a foundation upon which to build a whole theology. What exacerbates this error is the belief that the spirit is good while the soul and body are bad. The teaching then goes on to say that you must subdue the evil soul and the body, by means of the spirit, which is good. That assumption is based on an incorrect interpretation of Romans 7 and other passages of Scripture to mean that man has an inherent dual nature, a Jekyll and Hyde Syndrome.

It is also important to note that the word 'may' at the beginning of the verse wasn't in the original text and was added by translators. He wasn't speaking to an individual, but rather to the body of Thessalonian believers. This verse should read something like this: "The God of peace is the one who sets all of you apart completely. Your (the corporate body of believers) whole spirit, soul and body is preserved blameless until the coming of our Lord Jesus Christ. The one who calls you is faithful and He will preserve you."[4]

The Dualistic Mindset

The dual nature concept has resulted in thoroughly confusing believers all over the world by giving them an entirely incorrect interpretation of Romans 7, because it is generally believed that Paul discusses his dual nature in Romans 7. The thinking is that the Spirit and flesh are in a constant struggle inside us, yet in Romans 6 Paul told us that our sinful nature died. Since Romans 7 is after Romans 6, the assumption is that Paul superseded his teaching from Romans 6, then overrode and clarified in Romans 7 that we have two natures that struggle within us, the flesh and the spirit. And then the teaching is supposedly confirmed by references from other places in the Bible about Jacob and Esau and other passages.

In reality, Romans 7 should be read in the context of Romans 6. Paul spent an entire chapter explaining that our old nature died with Christ and that we were buried with Him. Then in Romans 7, he goes on to explain the struggle that we used to have under the law and goes on to say that Jesus has delivered us from that struggle. Paul would have to have been really schizophrenic if after going to such great lengths explaining to us so masterfully in Romans 6 that our old sin nature had died, he preached such a diametrically opposite doctrine in Romans 7. To interpret Romans 7 as saying that we have a dual nature defies all logic and common sense. Yet the entire church has swallowed this interpretation of Romans 7, hook, line and sinker.

In fact, in Romans 7:5-6 Paul speaks in past tense about our experience when we were sinners living under the law. He then goes on to explain in Romans 7:14-20 about the struggle we previously faced with our old sinful nature, before we came to Christ. You'll also want to note that Paul's narration is in present tense. It is quite common for a person explaining something to switch to the present tense when he really gets into his narration.[4]

My Salvation Experience

For example, here is how I came to a saving knowledge of Jesus Christ. Back in the early eighties I was up in the mountains of India when a beehive was somehow disturbed nearby and bees flew straight toward me. All of a sudden hundreds of bees are all over my face (Note the transition from past to present tense). I am paralyzed by fear, terrified that I could infuriate the bees and be stung. I can't even open my mouth to pray. At that moment, I pray the most desperate prayer of my entire life without even opening my mouth, because my mouth is covered with bees. I cry out to the Lord, asking Him to save me this once and promising that I would serve Him the rest of my life. It wasn't long before a bee stings me in the ear and I run as fast as I can for help. Before I knew it fourteen more bees sting me. Forty bee stings are usually fatal, so I was extremely thankful that He saved me from almost certain death. (Note the transition to past tense, much like Paul did in Romans 7:25).

Now, notice that I started the story in the past tense. As I got into the story, I switched to present tense for better narration. That is what Paul is doing. He starts Romans 7 in the past tense by explaining our state under the law. After that, he starts narrating the experience that man used to have while he was under the law in first person and in the present tense. At the end of Romans 7, he asks a hypothetical question in Romans 7:24, "What a wretched man I am! Who will rescue me from this body of death?" Then he provides the solution in Romans 7:25, "Thank God – He has done it through Jesus Christ our Lord" (William BECK translation).

Struggle Between the Spirit and Flesh?

Most believers think there is a constant struggle within them between the Spirit and the flesh. In fact, they think that their whole spiritual walk consists in subduing the flesh daily by means of the Spirit.

Galatians 5:16-17 says: "Walk in the Spirit, and you shall not fulfill the lust of the flesh. For the flesh lusts against the Spirit, and the Spirit against the flesh; and these are contrary to one another, so that you do not do the things that you wish."

This verse is often misconstrued to mean that the Spirit and the flesh are at odds within us. This verse is a favorite excuse for believers to say that they are schizophrenic with two natures. They therefore have a constant struggle with their flesh and use this as an excuse to sin.

This passage is actually saying just the opposite. It says you don't have a dual nature in you. Romans 8:7 (Mirror Bible)[6] tells us that the flesh (self-righteousness) and spirit (faith righteousness) are opposing forces. (Flesh no longer defines you—faith does!) .

The Spirit and flesh are two opposing entities. You either have the Spirit or you have the sinful nature. The two cannot exist simultaneously in the same person[4].

Romans 8:9 clearly tells us, "But you are not in the flesh but in the Spirit, if indeed the Spirit of God dwells in you."

Further down in Galatians 5, Paul further proves this interpretation in verse 24 (which is right after Galatians 5:17), "And those who are Christ's have crucified the flesh with its passions and desires."

If you have crucified the flesh, how could you possibly have two natures struggling within you? You have only the Spirit of God in your new nature that replaced the old man/old sinful nature. You are crucified with Christ. Paul uses the whole of Romans 6 to explain this truth to us. I didn't get this for thirty years!

Your old nature is dead! Your old self is gone! You don't have an old depressed self or a fearful self. Your new nature is filled with abundant, overflowing, joyful life. Your old, poor self is dead. You have no more lack. You are now united with the Triune God and all your needs are met in Him and through Him. Your old sick self is dead. You are now brimming with youthful vigor and perfect health. Jesus has delivered you from all your fear, sickness, shame, depression and poverty. You are now free from any form of sickness, depression, poverty, shame, fear or inadequacy of any kind. You can live a life that is always full of joy, health, boldness, love and prosperity. Why live in something that you have been totally delivered from?[4]

What is Sanctification?

There is a great deal of confusion in the church about sanctification. About ten years ago, I was on a quest for the true meaning of sanctification. I searched Amazon for books on the subject and read several that utterly confused me. In fact, my bookshelf is still stacked with them. If you asked the question "Is sanctification instantaneous or progressive?" you would hear Bible teachers offer a deep, esoteric revelation with a wise, inscrutable, know-it-all look on their faces, which no one, including them understands. They say, "Your sanctification started when you got saved. After that, sanctification is a lifelong process." They use the word sanctification to mean putting your sinful nature to death on a daily basis by means of the Spirit. But that isn't the meaning of sanctification at all! Sanctification (Greek word hagiazo) means 'set apart for God' or 'sacred'. You were sanctified once and for all when Jesus died on the cross and rose again[4].

1 Corinthians 1:30 says: "Christ Jesus became for us wisdom from God—and righteousness and sanctification and redemption."

A closely related topic is Perfection. I was on a quest for perfection. Keep this important truth in mind: Christian perfection means nothing more than to be one with Christ, who is perfect in every way, and this occurred when we were united with Christ through His death, burial and resurrection. You are now perfect because you are one with the perfect One! Now you can walk before Him perfect all the days of your life![4]

    I would encourage you to read John Crowder's masterpiece, Mystical Union[4], for a detailed treatment of this topic. This book provides the answer to almost every other passage of scripture that has been misinterpreted to mean that we have the dual nature. No other book deals with this subject so completely and masterfully. The truths in his book are irrefutable. If we don't get this truth settled in our heart, and understand all passages of scripture that we have incorrectly interpreted, we could find an excuse to sin.

Chapter 7: The Inclusion Question

In this chapter, I would like to address some questions about Inclusion, hoping that it will answer some concerns that may be out there.

Question 1: Are all forgiven by God?

Question 2: Are all reconciled to God?

Question 3: Are all saved?

What is Inclusion?

Everyone was created because God wanted to include them in the fellowship and intimacy enjoyed by Father, Son and Holy Spirit from before the foundation of the world.

Man was created with freedom of choice (not free will). Man sinned and was an enemy in his mind to God[1].

God came to seek and save mankind. Jesus came to earth as mankind, lived as mankind, and died as mankind. A brand new creation rose with Jesus when He rose from the dead[2]. All of mankind ascended with Him and is seated at the right hand of God. Jesus came as the last Adam, viz. the last man with the fallen sinful nature of Adam. The new creation has the image and likeness of God and has been restored to the image of the perfect Man[3], the Son of God. God single-handedly accomplished His plan of salvation without any help from man.

Man still needs to align with God's reconciliation and salvation in order to benefit from it.

Are All Forgiven by God?

Yes, God has forgiven all of mankind that has ever lived and that will ever live, of all their sins, past, present and future.

This happened during the Incarnation of Jesus. Jesus forgave all sins during his life on earth, on the cross and by His death and resurrection.

People who haven't come to a saving knowledge of Jesus Christ don't know this, and some of them don't care about it and are living in their sins. Others are performing works to appease their mental image of an angry God. The kind of works that people are performing is different, based on which religion they are following.

Even most people who have come to a saving knowledge of Jesus Christ are still living in guilt, shame and condemnation because of an incorrect understanding of the grace of God. There are many who don't have a proper understanding of the forgiveness of God.

Even though everyone is forgiven, most people, both unbelievers and believers are not really benefitting from it either because they don't know Jesus or they know Jesus and don't have a proper understanding of the forgiveness of God.

This has been covered extensively in different sections of this book.

Are All Reconciled to God?

Yes. God was in Christ reconciling the world to Himself. 2 Corinthians 5:19 says "God was in Christ reconciling the world to Himself, not imputing their trespasses to them, and has committed to us the word of reconciliation."

Those that haven't come to a saving knowledge of Christ may still be living in their sins because they don't know this. The word of reconciliation has been committed/entrusted to us. We bring the gospel of reconciliation to those who haven't come to a saving knowledge of Jesus Christ.

Now, even many of those that have come to a saving knowledge of Jesus Christ still don't believe that they have been reconciled. Many still think God is angry with them and is distant from them.

This too has been covered at length in different sections of this book.

Is Everyone Saved?

God has single-handedly accomplished our salvation without any help from man. Mankind has been brought into favor and accepted by God. Unless someone comes to a saving knowledge of Jesus Christ, they don't benefit from God's act of forgiveness, reconciliation and salvation.

For all three of the above questions, we have God's side and man's side. God has forgiven everyone, reconciled everyone and has accomplished the act of salvation without anyone's help. Man needs to come to an understanding of what God has done and believe to be able to benefit from what God has done.

God's Side

From God's side, He desired everyone and wanted everyone before the foundation of the world, and before we were conceived in our mother's womb[4]. He created every man, woman and child out of love and because He wanted them.

The act of the Incarnation was proof that God wanted every man, woman and child so badly that He came to earth seeking man (The Parables of the lost sheep, the lost coin and the Prodigal son in Luke 15). 1 Timothy 2:4 and 2 Peter 3:9 state that it is God's will for everyone to be saved and that no-one should perish and that all should come to repentance. John 3:16 says "For God so loved the world that He gave His only begotten Son, that whoever believes in Him should not perish."

Man still needs to come to a saving knowledge of Jesus to benefit from what God has done.

What Does Saved Mean?

The question is, what do we mean by believing in Him and what does the word 'saved' mean? The Greek word *Sozo* that is translated saved is a more wholesome word than what we have normally understood the word to mean. *Sozo* means saved, healed, delivered, set free, restored and complete, made whole, blessed and prospered.

Part of the problem with the controversy about inclusion is the understanding of the Greek word *Sozo*. *Sozo* has traditionally been interpreted to mean only spiritual salvation, which has been narrowly interpreted to mean that you go to heaven when you die. Traditional Christianity believes that our life in this world is short compared to eternity. So, they say that our focus should be on eternity and not on the fleeting aspects of this temporary existence. The picture that comes to mind in traditional Christian thinking when the word 'Saved' is mentioned is that you go to heaven when you die if you are saved. So the controversy about Inclusion is that Jesus came to earth and died for your sins. You are not 'saved' and don't get your ticket to heaven unless you say the prayer of salvation in Romans 10. This is a narrow perspective of salvation.

I explained in detail in the chapter on the Primary purpose of creation that you were created to be included in the Trinity for the purpose of intimacy with the Triune God. I explained in the chapter on the Incarnation that God created such a beautiful world for Himself. He has now united Himself with you and is enjoying the world with you and through you. I would suggest a re-reading of those two chapters if you are not convinced. Yes, it is true that you would also spend eternity with God if you come to a saving knowledge of Jesus. But God didn't create you here on this earth just so that you could die and go to heaven one day.

You were created for the purpose of inclusion when God first thought of you and then thought of you through eternity when He intricately designed you. Man departed from God. Jesus came to restore you back to His original design in the act of Incarnation. He came to seek and save the lost, which is every one of us. In the chapter on the Incarnation, I have explained in detail how all of creation, including you was in Him when He lived on earth. When He died, you died. When He rose, a new creation rose with Him. All of mankind was included in His life, death, burial, resurrection and ascension. Paul spent several chapters in Romans explaining this to us in excruciating detail. It is true that none of this is available to anyone unless one believes. You partake of the New Covenant in Christ.

Holistic Salvation

Jesus came so that we may have life and that we may experience it abundantly. Some of us believe for forgiveness of sins, but not for healing. Others don't believe for deliverance, provision and financial abundance. We haven't taken advantage of all the benefits of Salvation in the way God intended us to. We could say that some of us have been saved from a spiritual standpoint and that we are not saved from a physical, emotional and material standpoint.

As explained in detail in the Chapters 'Are you only 1/3 saved', 'Primary Purpose of Creation' and 'Incarnation', God's intent was union with man. He accomplished union with man in the Incarnation. Again, we need to believe and live in this Union. By 'Believe' I mean come to an understanding of, identify with, and get a revelation of, come to a knowing of and participate in union with God. We need to come to a knowing of the fact that we are united with God now and will be forever. Union with

God means we are crucified with Christ and it is no longer we who live, but Christ lives in us[7]. We need to know that this union includes spiritual union, healing, deliverance and financial abundance. When we know that we are always healed, we will always be healed. When we know that we are always full of His abundance and have no lack, we will experience it. When we know that we have the Oil of joy in us, we will be happy always.

What is Faith?

It is not our faith. It is His faith. Ephesians 2:8 says "For by grace you have been saved through faith, and that not of yourselves; it is the gift of God." It is the faith of God[6].

Faith is not a work. It is an effortless understanding, recognition, realization and knowing of what God has done for us and blending into and living in oneness with Him in the finished work of Christ.

What is Union with God?

Jesus prayed in John 17:21-24 that we might be one with God in the same way that the Triune God has been one through eternity. His prayer was a prayer of inclusion—for us to be included in the beautiful fellowship that the Triune God has been enjoying through eternity. Jesus accomplished this prayer through His life, death, resurrection and ascension. We are now included in the fellowship of the Triune God. We are now one with Father, Son and Holy Spirit, never to be separated from Him. He loves us so much that He would settle for nothing less than total and complete blending with every cell of our being [167]. Through the Incarnation, God accomplished His eternal goal and design of man. Now we have been brought into closest proximity with God. Immanuel is closer to us than the air we breathe. God doesn't exclude anyone. Man excludes himself by rejecting God.

Chapter 7: The Inclusion Question

How do We Live in Union with God?

Jesus said "I only do what I see the Father do." "I only say what I hear the Father say." He was describing His relationship of oneness with the Father. Now we are one with Him, included in the love-relationship of the eternal Triune God and in union with Him. Now the eternal Triune God is an integral part of our being. We live with Him, in Him and through Him. He lives in us and through us and is inseparable from us. Our life is an effortless life of understanding, recognizing, realizing and knowing that we are one with Him and living in that Oneness. Now we only say what we hear the Father say. We only do what we see the Father do. We just look into the mirror of who we are, the image and likeness of the perfect Man. We live spontaneously out of the fullness of our oneness with God. This is the glorious life that we have been designed for, a life of intimacy in ecstatic union with the Triune God.

The last chapter of this book, Effortless Living in His Amazing Grace is devoted to the intricate details of living in Union with Him.

Grace and Inclusion

Union with God (Inclusion) is an integral part of the Grace message. Relationship with God and union with Him are the essential factors that make grace work. In fact, I believe that this could be the balance that opponents of the gospel of grace are looking for. This is the other side of the grace coin.

It has been my intention to present the full, balanced, complete gospel of Jesus Christ in this book. Once we understand the big picture, the true gospel is irrefutable.

Chapter 8: Living Under an Open Heaven

If you have read this far and stop reading now, you'll miss the whole point of the book. You've probably heard of Open Heaven conferences with the theme being praying and doing spiritual warfare till we get an open heaven. Then, by the end of the conference, after praying, binding and loosing, we think we have attained an open heaven.

What is an open heaven? What do you need to do to get an open heaven? What is the result of an open heaven? What was the result of the Ascension of Jesus?

You have probably heard people preach or teach in favor of or against the grace message primarily from the perspective of sin and forgiveness. But the reality is that the grace message is the entire gospel. It is not just about forgiveness of sins. I am presenting the big picture to you. We have looked at why God created the heavens and the earth, and now we have a better understanding of why God created human beings. We know why Jesus came to earth. Quite often, when we talk about the Incarnation, we talk just about the crucifixion and the resurrection. We don't hear much taught on the topic of Jesus living on our behalf. We also don't hear much about what was accomplished when Jesus ascended to heaven.

The revelation of an Open Heaven has revolutionized my life and brought me into a level of freedom that I didn't think was possible. If you hang with me for the next few pages, your life too will be revolutionized. We will review the mechanism by which you can release God's amazing grace into your life and into the lives of those around you.

Introduction to an Open Heaven

When Jacob was on his way to his Uncle Laban's house, he had an encounter with God at a place that he called Bethel. He had a dream where angels of God were ascending and descending to heaven. His response was, "Surely, the Lord is in this place¹. This is another of my favorite scriptures. He goes on to say in the next verse "How awesome is this place! This is none other than the house of God, and this is the gate of heaven."

Jacob momentarily experienced a portal into heaven. He had a glimpse into a gateway to heaven. The angels of God were probably ascending and descending upon him at other times too. Jacob saw how angels of God were ministering to him, going up to heaven with his cries and desires and bringing back the realities of heaven to him on earth.

Jesus Obtained Access to an Open Heaven

Jesus tells Nathaniel in John 1:50 "Most assuredly, I say to you, hereafter you shall see heaven open, and the angels of God ascending and descending upon the Son of Man."

What did Jesus mean when He said 'hereafter'?

In Matthew 3:16-17 we see the heavens open: "When He had been baptized, Jesus came up immediately from the water; and behold, the heavens were opened to Him, and He saw the Spirit of God descending like a dove and alighting upon Him. And suddenly a voice came from heaven, saying, 'This is My beloved Son, in whom I am well pleased.'"

The heavens have been open ever since! In the Incarnation, we saw that Jesus came as man, representing all mankind. His baptism represented mankind's baptism. When you get baptized, you identify with His act of baptism.

Isaiah's prayer in Isaiah 64:1 (NIV) was: "Oh that You would rend the heavens and come down". This prayer was fulfilled by the Incarnation of Jesus. The heavens were opened to Jesus, and angels of God ascended and descended upon Jesus from that time on. Jesus brought the treasures of heaven to every person He encountered. He healed blind eyes, deaf ears and lame people. Jesus fed multitudes of people supernaturally, cast out demons, and raised the dead—all through this open heaven that was over Him. Jesus lived under an open heaven. In fact, Jesus was an open heaven, and He has been an open heaven ever since.

The Veil that Separated Us from God

We read in Matthew 27:50-51 that Jesus said "It is finished." And Jesus cried out again with a loud voice, and yielded up His spirit. Then, behold, the veil of the temple was torn in two from top to bottom."

God ripped open the veil in the temple from top to bottom, signifying that it was done supernaturally without the help of man. God provided us an open heaven, all by Himself. The veil that separated man from God was torn in two and there is no longer a veil between man and God. Now we live in the finished tense (a phrase coined by Mike Miller, The Father's House Ministries) under an open heaven. We don't have to fast and pray for hours on end for the heavens to open. The heavens are already open to us. We pray, not for the heavens to be opened, but because we love Him and want to spend time with Him.

2 Corinthians 3:18 says: "But we all, with unveiled face, beholding as in a mirror the glory of the Lord, are being transformed into the same image from glory to glory, just as by

the Spirit of the Lord."

We now have access to the glory of the Lord with nothing to separate us from Him. Moses was the only man in the Old Testament who could see God face to face. But in reality God's intent has always been for all of us to see Him face to face. Now you and I can see God face to face every moment of every day, with nothing separating us from Him.

We as human beings are often separated from our loved ones. A husband and wife are separated from each other and their children from morning to evening when they go to work. Sometimes they are separated from each other for a few days or a few weeks for various other reasons. Just as we miss our loved ones very much when we are separated from them, God never desired any separation from man. He has always wanted to be with man, close to him every moment of every day, and He accomplished that with His Incarnation. God is with you, in you, every moment of every day, never again to be separated from you. He is with you in everything you do, always loving on you and caring for you! You never need to experience another moment of separation from the One who loves you more than anyone has ever loved you—the lover of your soul!

Did God Turn His Face from Mankind?

We saw earlier in Colossians 1:21 that: "And you, who once were alienated and enemies in your mind by wicked works, yet now He has reconciled."

God never turned His face from mankind. Rather we tend to hide our faces from Him because of the shame and guilt we feel because of our sin. Jesus has removed that veil so we can now see clearly—that every person is now reconciled to God. This is the gospel that we need to preach to those who don't know Jesus and are living in bondage out of ignorance.

2 Corinthians 5:19 says, "that God was in Christ reconciling the world to Himself, not imputing their trespasses to them, and has committed to us the word of reconciliation"

Now, each and every one of us needs to come to a saving knowledge of Jesus Christ and walk in His saving grace to reap the full benefits of what He has done. This is important for our physical, emotional and mental wellbeing as well as that of our loved ones.

Heaven has Invaded Earth

And then we read in Acts 2:1-4: "When the Day of Pentecost had fully come, they were all with one accord in one place. And suddenly there came a sound from heaven, as of a rushing mighty wind, and it filled the whole house where they were sitting. Then there appeared to them divided tongues, as of fire, and one sat upon each of them. And they were all filled with the Holy Spirit and began to speak with other tongues, as the Spirit gave them utterance."

There was a rushing mighty wind because of the open heaven; heaven that was ripped open during Jesus' time on earth to remove all barriers and impediments between God and man. Heaven has invaded earth so that God is no longer separated from us. Now His amazing grace is all yours, no holds barred!

Jesus is Immanuel, God with us. He has sent Holy Spirit to earth, who is now with us. No more veil of separation! God has achieved what He always wanted, closeness, nearness and togetherness with man. Yet we have strayed so far from the truth that people are writing bumper stickers and songs like: "Jesus is coming and, boy, is He pissed." Most of the church thinks the devil is taking over, and is waiting for the Rapture, God's big government bailout program.

Chapter 8: Living Under an Open Heaven

In His Image

Athanasius's doctrine of divinization says this: "'The Word 'was made man so that we might be made God." Athanasius used the word *theopoie*. Literally, this word means 'to make God' or, more politely, 'to make divine.' God has restored us to the place of righteousness and innocence, to the place He originally intended for us, in His image and His likeness.

Jesus said in John 10:34: "Is it not written in your law, 'I said, "You are gods."'"

Dogs communicate with dogs, cats communicate with cats and lions communicate with lions. Who does God communicate with? Dogs can't communicate effectively with cats or lions or humans the way they can with other dogs. God didn't create us to be a species of pet that He could take care of and clean up after. Throughout this book, I have emphasized the point that God created us for intimate fellowship with Him. That is why God created man in His image and likeness.[2]

God created man to be just like Him, not just in heaven sometime in the future, but right here during our life on earth so that He could live in us and through us, united with us. Now what would be the point of creating us to be like Him and then leaving us on our own to live life with our meager power and abilities? Well, guess what? Jesus came to earth as man, on behalf of man. Jesus lived as man, on behalf of man. When He was baptized, He was baptized on your behalf. When you were baptized, you identified with His act of baptism. When God said: "This is my beloved Son in whom I am well pleased" He was saying it to you[3].

You are a Living Open Heaven

There is nothing separating you from God, not your sin,

guilt or shame. From God's point of view you are righteous, holy and perfect always. Jesus has torn the veil. He has removed everything that was between you and God. You never need to feel guilt or shame at any time of your life. Just walk in who you are, in the image and likeness of God!

When the heavens opened above Jesus, they opened above you. When Jesus died, you died. When Jesus rose from the dead, you rose with Him as part of the new creation. You have the same open heaven that Jesus had: He has given us an open heaven. To take it a step further, you are an open heaven! Angels of God are descending and ascending upon Jesus. Christ is in you. You are united with Christ. Angels of God are descending and ascending from heaven to you right this moment.

You have access to heaven. You have access to everything that God has—to His heavenly treasures. Jesus cast out demons, healed the sick and raised the dead. In Mark 16, He tells us to cast out demons and lay hands on the sick. That is because the heavens that opened up to Him are now open to us.

In Revelation 4:1, we read about the door standing open in heaven. This is the door that was open when Jesus was baptized and has been open ever since. The voice from Revelation 4:1 is asking us to come up there. Now we will see how we can go up through the door, reach out to the treasures in heaven and bring them down to earth. We can go back and forth, up and down through that open door in heaven at will. We are channels from heaven to earth, conduits of all God's blessings to our lives and the lives of those around us. This is our mission here on earth: to make earth like heaven.

In Genesis 1:28, God's mission to man was to subdue the earth. He created Eden as a slice of heaven, a place where heaven and earth intersected. His mission to man was to make the rest of the earth like Eden.

That mission hasn't changed. Jesus teaches us how to pray in Matthew 6:10 and asks us to pray "Thy kingdom come, Thy will be done, on earth as it is in heaven." It is God's will that earth become like heaven. God's mission to man has always been to make earth like heaven.

Keys to the Kingdom of Heaven

Okay, now let's see how this works. We have been living with our limited abilities all these years. So you must be thinking—"What are these heavenly treasures? How do I access them, and for what purpose?"

Matthew 16:19 tells us: "And I will give you the keys of the kingdom of heaven, and whatever you bind on earth will be bound in heaven, and whatever you loose on earth will be loosed in heaven."

Jesus has given you the keys to the kingdom of heaven! Whatever you bind on earth will be bound in heaven. The literal rendering of this verse would be: "And I have given you the keys to the kingdom of heaven, and whatever you bind on earth is already bound in heaven, and whatever you loose on earth is already loosed in heaven." The word for 'loosed' can also be translated as 'permit/allow.' The word for 'bind' can be translated as 'forbid/disallow.' So, here's how it works: You look to see what is permitted in heaven and you allow that on earth. You determine what is forbidden in heaven and you forbid it on earth. Let's turn this verse around. We've always thought that after we bind and loose on earth, it will be bound and loosed in heaven, but it is actually the other way around. We allow on earth what has already been allowed in heaven. We disallow on earth what has already been disallowed in heaven. We reach out to heaven and bring the treasures of heaven to earth because we have open, free heavenly access.

You are a Royal Priesthood

In Zechariah 3:6, the angel of God told Zechariah the priest that he had access to walk among the heavenly hosts. He told Zechariah that he had heavenly access.

1 Peter 2:9 says that we are a royal priesthood. We are His priests to whom He has given dominion over the earth. Until the late seventies I was a Hindu. In Hindu temples, the priests chant and perform rituals that most attendees cannot understand. I've never been to a Jewish synagogue, but from reading the Old Testament, I can imagine that it probably isn't much different there. I have attended traditional Christian churches on many occasions. There again, we see religious rituals performed, often to appease an angry God. Yet we have already seen that our God is not an angry God. We have also seen that He created us for the purpose of intimacy with Him and that we are in union with Him. In other words, you and I are not part of a priesthood that performs religious rituals to appease an angry God. You are a priest who worships and adores Him out of a heart of passionate love and gratitude. He has given you complete access to all that He has. This is your priestly role: you are seated with Him in the heavenlies, with His left arm under your head and His right arm embracing you.

Chapter 9: The Kingdom of God

Let's talk briefly about the revelation of the kingdom of God before we talk about the New Testament model of prayer. It wouldn't be fair to you if I said you didn't need to fast and pray for hours to get God to bless you, and not mention the New Testament Prayer model. We need a revelation of the kingdom and dominion to enable us to understand the model of prayer.

Genesis 1:28 has always been God's kingdom model, commanding us to fill the earth, subdue it and have dominion.

God created Eden, a slice of heaven. Eden wasn't just a garden with lush vegetation and sweet, juicy fruit. Eden was a place where heaven and earth met. Heaven and earth were one in Eden. Eden was a place of perfect happiness, filled with the glory of God. Once Adam and Eve left the garden, cherubim guarded the way to the Tree of Life so that they wouldn't eat of it and live forever in their fallen state of sin and sickness. If someone got cancer, God didn't want him to live forever in the fallen state, suffering with cancer. Cherubim are often mentioned in the Bible in conjunction with the glory of God. God placed Adam in Eden and asked him to fill the earth, subdue it, have dominion over it and make the rest of earth like Eden, the model/prototype of heaven. God asked Adam to extend the boundaries of Eden to cover the whole earth.

Ever-Increasing Kingdom

We read in Isaiah 9:6 that the government would be upon His shoulders. Isaiah 9:7 says: "Of the increase of His government and peace there will be no end."

I am a part of one of the largest prophetic and teaching ministries in India. Before I came to the U.S. in 1990, I used to teach the Word of Faith message in spiritual warfare seminars as part of this ministry. I attended a prophetic church in Tampa from 1994 to 1998 and have attended numerous prophetic conferences. The general thought in some prophetic circles is that the world is getting worse and worse; pornography is on the increase, violence is everywhere and God is fighting a losing battle. So we think He needs our help. We think that that our job is to fast and pray to help God overcome the devil. So we hear doom and gloom prophecies about earthquakes and hurricanes in the areas that we think the devil is gaining a foothold, in places like Los Angeles and New Orleans.

But that is not what we see in Isaiah 9:6 and 7. The government is upon His shoulders and of the increase of His kingdom and peace there will be no end.

Habakkuk 2:14 says this: "For the earth will be filled with the knowledge of the glory of the Lord, as the waters cover the sea."

The kingdom of God is an ever-increasing kingdom and the knowledge of the glory of God shall fill the earth as waters cover the sea. We do not have an ever-decreasing kingdom that we have to somehow prop up with our fasting, prayer and spiritual warfare to help a powerless, impotent God. He is the almighty, omnipotent God. Well, here's how we could help: we could stop declaring and decreeing doom and gloom and spreading the lie that the devil is taking over the world. It is almost fashionable in some Christian circles to get on stage and talk about how the devil is doing so much damage. It is then followed by the statement that God is more powerful and that we can pray and defeat the devil. The amazing truth is that Jesus has already defeated the devil. A lot of folks are of an Old Testament mindset that the heavens over their little village or town are like brass and that the demons in their area are a special kind of evil super-spirit.

In Daniel 2, Daniel explains King Nebuchadnezzar's dream. He describes the head of gold, chest and arms of silver, belly and thighs of bronze, legs of iron and feet partly of iron and partly of clay. He goes on to explain that different kingdoms with varying levels of glory will dominate the earth one after another. In Daniel 2:44-45, Daniel tells us: "And in the days of these kings the God of heaven will set up a kingdom which shall never be destroyed; and the kingdom shall not be left to other people; it shall break in pieces and consume all these kingdoms, and it shall stand forever."

Daniel says that the kingdom of God will consume all other kingdoms and stand forever. Like everything else, most of the church pushes this off to the millennium. This is talking about the kingdom of God that was proclaimed by Jesus and has invaded the earth from the time the heavens were opened when Jesus was here on earth. It's important to note here that Jesus preached the kingdom all through the gospels. Jesus started His ministry by saying the Kingdom of God is at hand, meaning it is within reach. In another place He said the Kingdom of God is within you.

New Testament Kingdom Revelation

We see in Acts 1:3 that Jesus appeared to them over a period of forty days and spoke about the kingdom of God.

Paul also preached the kingdom of God. Acts 19:8 says that Paul entered the synagogue and spoke boldly there for three months, arguing persuasively about the kingdom of God.

In Acts 20:25 Paul says: "Now I know that none of you among whom I have gone about preaching the kingdom will ever see me again." At the end of his ministry, Paul says the focus of his preaching was the kingdom.

When the Greeks and Romans conquered a nation, they

would send in a team whose leaders were called apostles. This occurred even before the time of Christ. Their job was to transform the culture of that new country to be exactly like the culture of Greece or Rome. They would influence the lifestyle and even the architecture of the buildings of the conquered country to be like that of their own country. As a result, all countries in the Greek and Roman empires had the same unified culture.

Jesus preached the kingdom. He asked us to pray in Matthew 6:10 that His kingdom would come to earth. It is our responsibility to influence the culture of this world that we live in to be like the culture of heaven. This is our apostolic mission, similar to the mission of the teams led by apostles that the Greeks and Romans sent to influence the culture of conquered nations. What a difference we would see in our culture if we were all walking the kingdom walk, living the kingdom life and speaking kingdom talk, releasing heaven wherever we go.

Dr. Myles Munroe says this: "The Creator's intent was to administrate earth government from Heaven through His image (nature) in man and thus manifest His nature and character on earth."[1]

The Seven Spheres of Society

In 1975, God simultaneously gave Bill Bright, founder of Campus Crusade, and Loren Cunningham, founder of Youth with a Mission, a message. The message was that if we are to impact any nation for Jesus Christ, we would have to affect the seven spheres, or mountains of society that are the infrastructure of any society. These seven mountains are business, government, media, arts and entertainment, education, the family and religion.

More recently, a survey was done in Dallas, the most churched city in the U.S. to determine the impact made on the various areas of society. It was found that the areas of society other than religion were least impacted in Dallas, compared to other cities in the U.S. The church has done a pretty good job influencing the religion sphere of society. But we have not made any significant dent in other sections of our culture. Let's say we are totally successful in leading everyone to Christ. Would we be able to say that we have brought the Kingdom of God to earth? No-it is our responsibility to bring the Kingdom of God to every aspect of our culture.

Jesus said we are the light of the world. We are the salt of the earth. The general thought in the church is that we are doing something significant for God only if we are preaching the gospel and winning souls for Christ. The thought is that the rest of the members of a church are pew-sitters who fund those who win souls. The truth is that every one of us is a slice of heaven, an open heaven, wherever we go. We bring light and life to people in our everyday lives through our normal interactions. God has positioned us in the seven mountains of society. Through our life of union with God, together with God, we influence our culture and bring heaven to every aspect of our culture.

Heaven is the Standard, Jesus is the Model

Gen 1:28 tells us about our role as kings to be fruitful, multiply, subdue and take dominion on earth. Matthew 16:19, Zechariah 3:6 and 1 Peter 2:9 tell us about our priestly access.

As priests, we access the heavenly treasures and as kings, we bring them to earth. This is what Jesus did. He reached out to heaven in His priestly role and brought healing to everyone around Him in His kingly role. Jesus preached the truth of bringing heaven to earth.

It is now our responsibility to make earth like heaven. There is no sickness, anxiety or fear in heaven. Romans 14:17 says: "For the kingdom of God is not eating and drinking, but righteousness and peace and joy in the Holy Spirit." It is our responsibility to bring God's healing, righteousness, joy, peace and all other heavenly blessings to earth through the divine strategies that He gives us.

Heaven is the standard for what God wanted earth to be like. Hebrews 1:3 says that Jesus was the brightness of His glory and the express image of His person. Jesus is the model for what God desires and how to bring heaven to earth.

The Tree of Life

Now let's look at this same truth from a different angle.

In Revelation 22:1-2, John talks about the tree of life. "And he showed me a pure river of water of life, clear as crystal, proceeding from the throne of God and of the Lamb. In the middle of its street, and on either side of the river, was the tree of life, which bore twelve fruits, each tree yielding its fruit every month. The leaves of the tree were for the healing of the nations."[ii]

In heaven, John saw the tree of life that bore fruit every month, whose leaves were for healing.

Ezekiel saw the same river in Ezekiel 47:12: "Along the bank of the river, on this side and that, will grow all kinds of trees used for food; their leaves will not wither, and their fruit will not fail. They will bear fruit every month, because their water flows from the sanctuary. Their fruit will be for food, and their leaves for medicine."

In Revelation, John saw the Tree of Life in heaven with leaves for healing. Ezekiel saw many trees of life by the river.

Chapter 9: The Kingdom of God

The trees that Ezekiel saw also had leaves for healing. John saw Jesus as the Tree of Life in heaven and Ezekiel saw you and me and all others as trees of life here on earth.

Jesus says in John 12:24: "Unless a grain of wheat falls into the ground and dies, it remains alone; but if it dies, it produces much grain."

When Jesus died and rose again, all of mankind died and rose with Jesus, with the image and nature of Jesus. The death and resurrection of Jesus produced a species of god-humans just like Jesus. Jesus was 100% God and 100% man. You are 100% man and 100% God. Please refer back to how I explained man's technology that can transfer a whole library of books through a USB stick to a computer and then many computers. God has placed His fullness in you[5]. You have all of God and not just a little bit of God in you.

Obviously, you are not Omniscient, Omnipresent or Omnipotent. Luke 2:52 says Jesus increased in wisdom and stature. In the same way, we grow in the knowledge of Him. Of the many options God had when creating man, He chose a set of options. He created man in His image and likeness with freedom of choice without fore knowledge, uniquely for the purpose of intimate fellowship with Him, for God to live our lives here with us.

I have heard many versions of this truth. Some people have this revelation of His fullness. But they always fall short of describing the real awesomeness of this truth. They either say you are a little Jesus or that God came into little you. There is no little when it comes to Jesus! You are no longer little after God has come into you! Now you are no longer just you. You are now you, Father, Son and Holy Spirit. You no longer have just a first and last name. You can consider yourself as having a five-part name: Your first name, the name of tri-une God and then your last name. Let's say your first name is John and your last name is Smith. Your five-part name would be John Father Son Holy Spirit Smith. My five-part name would be Ravi Father Son Holy Spirit Durairaj. You are God's address. You are living and enjoying the Great Dance wherever you go, swirling around with Father, Son and Holy Spirit. You are dancing the great Dance, spreading the true gospel of Jesus Christ with everything you say and everything you do, wherever you go.

You as God

Christ in you the hope of glory[4] is an awesome truth. Another great truth is 'you as God'. Jesus came to earth as you. He lived as you and died as you. When He rose from the dead, you rose with Him as a new creation. When He ascended, you ascended. You are now seated at God's right hand together with Him. Now the prayer of Jesus in John 17 for you to become one with the Godhead has been accomplished. No one has seen God at any time. Jesus came to reveal God. We saw the verses where if you have seen Jesus you have seen the Father. Jesus came as the perfect expression of God[6]. Now, with the Incarnation, you and the Godhead have become one. Now, you are the perfect representation of the Godhead. John 4:17 says "as He is, so are we in this world."

As you are now one with the Godhead, when someone sees you, they see God. We are ambassadors of Christ. So just as Jesus came to earth as you, you are now here on earth as God! You are here as you and the fullness of God! Just as Moses was as God to Pharaoh[7], you are as God to the people you encounter in your everyday life. In the time of Moses, only he was as God to Pharaoh and Egypt. Now, every one of us is as God to the people and leaders of our society! We have had the following revelation for years: God is in us, God is with us, God is upon us and God is around us. 'You as God' is a powerful revelation that includes Christ in you! Let us walk in the fullness of this truth.

Kings and Priests

So, putting together Matthew 16:19 and what we saw in Ezekiel and Revelation, we look at the Tree of Life—Jesus—and see that He has healing in His wings. Malachi 4:2 says, "The Sun of Righteousness shall arise with healing in His wings." We reach out into heaven as priests, let the Sun of righteousness rise within us and release the healing in His wings. We bring the healing to earth as kings, to us, our family and to those around us. Whatever we see in heaven, we allow on earth. We allow healing because we see it in Jesus, the tree of life with healing in His wings.

Heaven is the standard, and there is no sickness in heaven. Jesus only healed the sick. He didn't bring sickness on anyone. Jesus is the model. As sickness is forbidden in heaven, we also forbid it on earth.

When we look at Jesus we see love. As priests, we must reach out and access His love that is freely available to us and release it on earth as kings. Love is available in heaven. Bring that love down to earth by loving everyone you come in contact with in your everyday life. Romans 5:5 tells us: "The love of God has been poured out in our hearts by the Holy Spirit who was given to us." 1 John 4:8 says "God is love." This is how we know that love is permitted in heaven. Heaven is the standard for love. Jesus is the compassionate model for the very love of God.

Jesus said: "The son of Man didn't come to be served, but to serve." So we live a life of service to those around us.

Nowhere does Scripture say that anger or hate is allowed in heaven, because it would be inconsistent with the character of

God. In fact, Matthew 5:22 (NIV) explains it this way: "But I tell you that anyone who is angry with a brother or sister will be subject to judgment." Some translations say: " . . . if you are angry without a cause." But the phrase 'without a cause' isn't in the original text. Because some translators thought it impossible to never be angry, they added the phrase 'angry without a cause'. "It's much like saying: "He who looks at a woman to lust after her without a cause"—which, obviously, is ludicrous. Anger isn't permitted in heaven. God swore in Isaiah 54:9 that He would never be angry with us again. So we are not to be angry with our brothers and sisters here on earth.

We look at the holiness of Jesus and realize that we have been created holy and blameless in His image. So we live holy and blameless and influence those around us to be holy and blameless. That is how we bring the holiness of heaven to earth.

There is no guilt, shame, insecurity or fear in heaven. Jesus has delivered us from these things in the here and now. When we live a lifestyle that is free from guilt, shame, insecurity and fear, we will impact those in our area of influence.

We look at Jesus and we see that He is Wisdom! Then we realize that we have the same wisdom. 1 Corinthians 1:30 explains: "But of Him you are in Christ Jesus, who became for us wisdom from God—and righteousness and sanctification and redemption." We get the revelation that we have access to His perfect wisdom! He gives us divine strategies in everything we do and makes us successful so that we can release His favor on everyone around us.

In one of his books, John Crowder says we are 'in-between creatures.'[3] We live in-between heaven and earth. We are in two places at once. We are divine conduits for the angels of God that are ascending and descending upon us, releasing the treasures of heaven on the people around us on earth. We are an open heaven! You are an open heaven! The Kingdom of God is heaven on earth. Just as Eden was a slice of heaven where heaven meets earth, you are now a slice of heaven where heaven meets earth. You are heaven on earth. God's mandate in Genesis 1:28 to take dominion and subdue the earth hasn't changed. You take the heaven in you and spread it to earth. When all of us do this, all of earth becomes heaven.

Today is the fifth day of the Holy Ghost Explosion. After I shared this yesterday, a lady came up to me and told me that she thought we go to heaven someday. I explained to her that eternal life and heaven start the day we come to a saving knowledge of Jesus. The Great Dance with you, Father, Son and Holy Spirit is heaven here on earth. It continues every day of your life on to when you step out of this body.

If you have watched Star Gate movies, when someone steps into the Star Gate, they are instantly transported to a different universe, sometimes into a different time. We are suspended between heaven and earth! We have access to everything in heaven. Our mandate is to bring it to earth and make earth like heaven.

Philippians 3:20 (NLT) says we are citizens of heaven. 2 Corinthians 5:20 says we are ambassadors for Christ. We represent God here on earth. We are citizens of heaven representing heaven as ambassadors to the people on earth who don't know Jesus.

Big God little devil

The traditional prayer model has been one of trying to persuade a reluctant God to unclench his hands and release His blessings. Or, it has been one of battling the principalities, the powers and the rulers in the heavenlies to defeat them, based on an Old Testament revelation from Daniel 10:13: "But the prince of the kingdom of Persia withstood me twenty-one days." I have great news for you: The devil has already been defeated! Jesus came here for this very purpose. 1 John 3:8 goes on to say: "For this purpose the Son of God was manifested, that He might destroy the works of the devil." It is one and done!

Hebrews 2:14 says "Inasmuch then as the children have partaken of flesh and blood, He Himself likewise shared in the same, that through death He might destroy him who had the power of death, that is, the devil"

In Daniel 7:13, we read: "And behold, One like the Son of Man, coming with the clouds of heaven! He came to the Ancient of Days, and they brought Him near before Him. Then to Him was given dominion and glory and a kingdom."

This took place during the ascension of Jesus. We hear a lot about the death and resurrection of Jesus, but not so much about His ascension. Verse 14 goes on to say that His dominion is an everlasting dominion. Then as we read on, it talks about the beast and how the authority of the devil was taken from him and given to the saints (verse 22, 27). The dominion has now been given to the saints. In Matthew 28:18, Jesus says He has all authority in heaven and on earth. He then went on to delegate that authority to us.

A major portion of the church has incorrectly relegated Daniel 7 to the millennium. In reality, Daniel 7 was fulfilled during the ascension of Jesus. The devil's authority has been stripped from him and given to us, the holy people. The kingdom of God, in like manner has been given to us, the holy people[8].

Adam was given authority in the Garden. At that point the devil had absolutely no authority. The devil knew the only way he could grab power was if he came to Adam to deceive him and steal his authority. Adam empowered the devil simply by falling for his lies.

Jesus defeated the devil and said He has all authority. What does that mean? If Jesus had all authority, the devil had none. In Matthew 28 and Mark 16, Jesus gave us the authority just as God gave Adam the authority. The only way the defeated devil, who has no authority, could have any authority would be by deceiving us, who have the authority. The devil would have authority only if we believed that he had any authority. The church has played right into the devil's hands and believed that he has authority and power. By believing the devil, the body of Christ is actually giving place to the activity of the enemy in their lives. In fact, the church has believed the lie of the enemy to such a degree that we hold numerous spiritual warfare conferences and write endless books on the subject. We credit the devil with power he simply doesn't have.

Whatever you focus on, you magnify. Whatever you magnify, you empower. Focusing on the devil makes him appear very big and powerful. We see him in everything instead of seeing God.[2]

Why rebuke the devil all day when you can just stop agreeing with him? That is why Ephesians 4:27 tells us not to give him any place.

All spiritual warfare boils down to truth versus lies. Not demons versus angels or God versus the devil. Not even us versus the devil. How is it warfare if the opposing side has already been defeated? Warfare implies we are trying to get victory. Jesus has already accomplished the victory. We are simply choosing to believe truth that sets us free and walk in the victory already afforded by the finished work of Jesus.

Ephesians 6 is a classic passage where devil is not

capitalized because it is not a proper noun. It is an adjective. It is describing something about a noun. It says stand against the wiles (cunning arts, deceit, craft, and trickery) of the devil. Devil means: prone to slander, slanderous, accusing falsely, a calumniator, false accuser, slanderer.

This passage tells us to stand against the tricks and deceit of the one who is always slandering and falsely accusing us. The same word is used in 1 Timothy 3:11, 2 Timothy 3:3 and Titus 2:3 of people who slander and accuse.

Ephesians 6 is not talking about warring against the devil. It is talking about standing firm against the tricks, lies and accusations of the one who slanders.

You may think that verse 12 says we wrestle with the principalities, powers and rulers. When we look at it in context starting in verse 11, it says—stand against the tricks, lies and accusations of the one who slanders. The people (flesh and blood) accusing or coming against us are not the enemy. They are victims of the lying spiritual forces influencing their minds.

The Greek word for armor is made up of 2 words:

1. Every and

2. Tool, instrument, weapon.

It simply means full equipment. It is metaphoric and refers to everything that Christ has made available through His finished work, namely, salvation, righteousness, peace, faith, etc.

James says resist the devil. The opposite of the Greek word for resist in James is to be in symphony with. James is telling us not to be in agreement or symphony with the devil. It is not telling us to resist him in spiritual warfare. It is telling us to resist him in our agreement. It is telling us to stop agreeing with his schemes and lies. There are weapons of our warfare

Chapter 9: The Kingdom of God

according to 2 Corinthians 10:3-5. It is to pull down strongholds, which are ways of thinking that are not in symphony with the mind of Christ.

Francois Du Toit said: "We have preached a defeated devil back into business."[10]

C. S. Lewis said "If I took the devil completely out of my theology, my theology would still stand."

Jesus cast out the legion of demons from the demoniac with one word 'Go.' Jesus is our model.

The problem is that most of us credit the devil with far more importance than he deserves. Smith Wigglesworth was awakened one day by an ominous presence. He opened his eyes to see Satan himself standing by his bedside. Wigglesworth said, "Ah, it is just you." He then turned over and went right back to sleep.

If you think the devil is in everything, you enable him to manifest in different areas of your life. Now, there are some wonderful healing and deliverance ministries like *Sozo* Ministries whose focus is on a big God and a little devil. People are restored by getting to the root of the issues that hinder their personal connection with Father, Son and Holy Spirit.

Prayer Model

Our prayer model is very simple. We declare and decree to bring to earth what we see in heaven. We see healing in heaven. We declare healing to those around us and ourselves. We see that there is no sickness in heaven, so we forbid sickness on earth. We speak to the sickness and cause it to cease to exist.

We see abundance in heaven. We declare and decree abundance here on earth. God gives us divine strategies that we use to release abundance into our lives and to those around us.

We realize we have an open heaven. Our God is a good, loving, and merciful God who has already blessed us abundantly with everything that we could possibly need. He desires nothing but goodness and abundance for us. We just thank Him for His blessings and walk in them. We expect nothing but goodness and abundance from Him in everything. His hand of favor is constantly outstretched toward us. We release all His blessings to everyone around us by what we say and do.

We don't have to limit this to our prayer time. All day long, we speak and release His Word that cannot return void no matter where we go[2]. When you speak, it is not just you speaking. *Rhema* originates with Father in you. You and He plan and think it through. You, together with Jesus, Word made flesh in you express the *Rhema*. Holy Spirit broods over everything you say and creates it. This is how you, Father, Son and Holy Spirit are living epistles, creating heaven and history. Every word you say is a prayer. You, Father, Son and Holy Ghost are saying it together.

Chapter 10: Effortless Living in His Amazing Grace

In this chapter, we will talk about effortless kingdom living, not by our efforts, but by His wonderful grace.

Have you ever felt that life is too hard? You wake up in the morning, go to work, do your best every day, only to return home and take care of your spouse and kids. Are you tired of the never-ending treadmill you're on? Do you wonder sometimes whether life could be better, whether there is a better way to live?

In John 15:11 Jesus said: "These things I have spoken to you, that my joy may remain in you, and that your joy may be full."

Jesus came to the earth and taught many things with one purpose—that your life might be full of joy! What do we want for our kids above anything else? We want them to be happy. We want to keep our spouse happy. Our whole life is geared toward this. In the same way, God, out of His immense love for us, wants us to be happy! He wants our joy to be full. He wants you to always overflow with joy. This is not a chapter on joy, so I won't quote all the scriptures that prove that God is a happy God and that He wants you to be happy. But to that end I highly recommend a book by Benjamin Dunn entitled 'The Happy Gospel.'

Let me ask you a question: Are you happy with life? If not, by the time you've finished reading this chapter, you will know how you can be happy.

There is a line of T-Shirts called 'Life is good.' Is your life good? If not, you can transform it.

I know many people who are stressed out, focused on nothing other than advancing their careers, riding that treadmill with no hope of getting off.

When I was a teen, a doctor told me that some people learn how to manage stress, while others never learn how to handle it and need medication to cope with it. Now if you need medication, please go ahead and take it. But I want you to know there is another way.

I have a young friend who just couldn't keep his job. He couldn't work eight hours a day without being overwhelmed by stress. Some people become overly stressed just from their commute to or from work. Some are fine as long as everything around them goes without a hitch and people treat them well. But their day is ruined the moment there is the slightest stressor. We were not designed to be controlled or ruled by our circumstances. God designed us to take authority over our circumstances.

Man has been on a constant quest for happiness and fulfillment. Does wealth bring happiness? No doubt you've heard about the miserable lives of some rich and famous people. Now, you can have all the money in the world; just don't let money have you. 1 Timothy 6:10 says "The love of money is the root of all evil." It doesn't say that money is the root of all evil. God has provided the means to happiness and fulfillment.

Enter His Rest

In Genesis 2:1-2, we read that after God was finished with creation, He rested.

In Hebrews 3 and 4, the Word of God encourages us to enter the rest of God.

In Matthew 11:28, Jesus tells us, "Come to Me, all you

Chapter 10: Effortless Living in His Amazing Grace

who labor and are heavy laden, and I will give you rest."

Here Jesus is referring to those who are living by their works, by their tedious, never-ending efforts. He says "I will give you rest." His rest is by His grace—His marvelous grace.

God created all things perfectly with the innate ability to repair and adjust. I will refer to this state of perfection that God created man in as the 'default state'. The 'default state' is the state of perfection that God created all things and all human beings in. If man strays from this perfect, natural, normal state, which I am calling the 'default state' of man, (s)he will automatically adjust to return to that state. Recently I hurt my finger while I was working out. Ten days later, I was amazed at my finger's ability to reproduce the damaged tissue and heal completely. My finger's default, perfect, natural, normal state is a state of healing. Within ten days, it reverted back to its default state.

Not too long ago, one of my relatives suffered cardiac failure. The doctors resuscitated him, performed a valve replacement and now, a month later, he is back at work, back to his default state of health and wholeness.

God has designed every part of man to live in healing. His default for us is healing and provision. That should be our expectation. We have to work hard to mess up that default state. And many of us do, through practicing unhealthy habits. Yet the truth is that when you expect sickness and lack you get exactly what you believe for.

God rested after creation in Genesis 2. He designed us to enter His provision in His rest and live effortlessly, not by our own works, but by His grace.

Our default state is innocence, holiness and righteousness. Many of us have strayed far from our default state into a fantasy world of addictions. The solution is to look in the mirror at our real innocent, holy, righteous self and keep on looking until we spontaneously realize that we are this beautiful innocent, holy, righteous person. And once that happens, we were designed to bounce right back into our innocent, holy, righteous default state.[2]

Our default state is happiness. Many of us have fallen into a delusional state of depression. Let us look into the mirror and see who we really are, the joyful person filled with the fullness of God, in total union with Him, overflowing with His abounding joy. As we gaze upon our true identity, joy unspeakable and full of glory will spontaneously rise up from within our true nature to overwhelm all the lies of sadness and depression.

When God rested after His creation, His Word continued to uphold all things. Hebrews 4:12 tells us that His Word is living and powerful. Isaiah 55:11 tells us that His Word doesn't return to Him void, but accomplishes what He pleases, and shall prosper in the thing for which He sent it.

The purpose of the Word is to automate everything that God created and ensure its design and sustenance. God's Word maintains everything in God's rest. We just need to believe (realize to be true) and enter God's rest. The Word of God created man in His image and likeness. Even though man fell, God's Word never fails, but accomplishes whatever He sent it to do. God's Word became flesh, reconciled man to God and restored God's original design of man by recreating him in His image.

By understanding certain principles of His kingdom, you can effortlessly live a life of excellence.

You were Designed to Live Effortlessly

God created the earth to give to you. The first river in

Chapter 10: Effortless Living in His Amazing Grace

Eden, *Pishon*, flows around a land that is filled with gold. Everything was designed to produce and give to man before the fall. Since the fall man has lived by the sweat of his brow, but Jesus has restored all that man lost through the fall. All that Jesus restored is available to man as he gets an understanding of what God has made available to him.

In his book 'Understanding Your Place in God's Kingdom', Author Myles Munroe said this in a section called: 'Your Original Purpose for Existence'—"The fall of mankind as recorded in the third chapter of Genesis was the result of man declaring independence from the government of heaven, resulting in anarchy and social and spiritual chaos. Ever since that fatal fall from governing grace, man has been attempting to establish a form of self-government that would alleviate the internal and external chaos he experiences. Of course, that chaos is also manifested in the natural physical creation he was mandated to govern—the earth." [1]

You don't have to live by the sweat of your brow anymore. You can live by His wonderful grace. Now, some of you are thinking that you don't need to work anymore, but that is not what I'm saying. Grace doesn't mean a free lunch. Grace doesn't mean you sit around on your couch, eating popcorn and cookies all day. It means living out of His fullness and not by your meager abilities.

In Romans 8:21-22, we read that all of creation groans for the revelation of the sons of God. Creation is waiting for us to be who we were created to be, so that it can produce and give to us the way it was originally designed to do.

Christ has redeemed us from the fallen state. Man is no longer in a fallen condition. All of creation is waiting for us to enter the rest that God has prepared for us to enjoy with Him.

Grace isn't Laziness

Before we look into how we can live in His rest, I want to digress a little and talk about spending our inheritance.

1 Corinthians 15:10 says this: "But by the grace of God I am what I am, and His grace toward me was not in vain; but I labored more abundantly than they all, yet not I, but the grace of God which was with me."

Paul, the author of this gospel of grace didn't just sit in his hammock and eat grapes all day. God's grace caused him to labor more abundantly than anyone else! How can you, who have such a huge inheritance from God, keep it to yourself?

Colossians 1:12 says "Giving thanks to the Father who has qualified us to be partakers of the inheritance of the saints in the light."

Ephesians 1:11 says something similar. God has given you His inheritance.

You have the secret of life through your faith in Jesus. How can you not, like Paul, be driven to share the gospel of His grace, the true gospel of Jesus Christ with everyone you meet?

After building one of the world's largest corporations and becoming the richest man in the world, Bill Gates realized that his life's pursuits were incomplete and far from fulfilling. As a result, he has committed almost his entire fortune to enhance health care and reduce extreme poverty around the world. This is the natural response of a human being who is entrusted with such great wealth.

The wealth that we have been entrusted with is worth far more than the combined wealth of Bill Gates and Warren Buffet. How much more should we share the true gospel of Jesus with the sick, poor and the needy around the world?

The gospel of grace isn't a 'Gimme, gimme, my name is Jimmy' gospel where we hoard everything the Lord has given us.

The whole gospel is about loving God, yourself and others. You will love yourself when you realize who you are. You will love others when you get a revelation of your purpose and inheritance.

The gospel isn't a 'name it and claim it', 'blab it and grab it' gospel, so that you, your spouse, your son and his spouse can live happily ever after. The church isn't a 'Bless Me' club.

I would also like to briefly expand on the prayer model that we saw in the previous chapter. Isaiah 28:11, 12 talk about entering His rest through praying in the Spirit. This is a vast subject and we won't go into the details here. But our prayer model also includes a lifestyle of praying in the Spirit and living in His rest.

Healthy and Whole

Now, let's see how you can live in His rest—how you can live in your inheritance.

So what is your inheritance? It is abundant and overflowing eternal life, which includes health, wealth, wisdom, love, joy, peace and much more right here on earth. It is not for the sweet by and by, in heaven, because there will be no need to be healed in heaven, as there is no sickness there. Nor is there any other kind of need or lack.

God has designed you and everything else He created to live in perfect health and heal automatically whenever anything tries to steal your health. This is God's rest for your body. I heard a message by Gloria Copeland in the early 80s that proved beyond a shadow of a doubt that it is God's will to heal you, that Jesus is God's will for healing in action, that you can be healed and speak healing to others.

Joseph Prince has a wonderful book, Health and Wholeness through the Holy Communion[2]. I endorse that book but take those truths further to say that when 1 Corinthians 11:29 talks about rightly discerning the Lord's body, it can be applied, not just during Communion, but every moment of every day to live a healthy life. You just need to rightly discern that when Jesus died, the old, sick you also died. When He rose, the new, healthy you rose with Him. The new you does not have the ability to get sick. If you get sick, it is because you believed and gave permission to a lie from an outside source. It is not impossible for you to get sick, but you don't have the ability within you to get sick. God created you to always be healthy by default. It is only because we don't know God's design for our health that we believe lies and end up getting sick like everyone else. Jesus has set you free from sickness and disease of every kind.

Here's the bottom line: this truth is not a secret that can only be enjoyed by a privileged few super-hero preachers. Everyone can appropriate this truth every day free of charge. This is a truth that has been quite popular for more than fifty years and has been available to us for more than 2000 years. We have no excuse to be sick. Now, I know that some folks have tried to put us into a guilt trip and say that if we are sick, it is because of lack of faith, but that isn't so. Go to a doctor if you are sick and take medicines until you are able to enter His rest in healing. You can live healed by always expecting to be who you have been created to be, healed and whole always. Don't expect to be sick. I know that most of the world lives in expectation of illness just like everyone else. It may be hard to change habits and expectations overnight, but as you start walking in this new revelation and keep on looking in the mirror, you will find that you will start transforming into the beautiful, healthy person that you are.

Who is the Wisest Person on Earth?

Let me ask you a question: Who is the wisest man who has ever lived? You will probably say Solomon, because that's what the Bible tells us. But would you agree with me that Jesus was wiser than Solomon? Jesus says in Matthew 12:42 that a greater than Solomon is here, referring to Himself.

Jesus is the wisest Man who ever lived. Now 1 Corinthians 1:30 tells us that Christ has become to us wisdom. Now, add to that Colossians 1:27 where it says: "Christ in us, the hope of glory." The wisest Man who ever lived lives in you! So you have the wisdom of Christ. What does that make you? The wisest (wo) man who has ever lived! He created you in His image, full of His wisdom! Isn't that mind-boggling?

Okay, now how do you enter His rest in wisdom? It is simple. Galatians 2:20 tells us: "I have been crucified with Christ; it is no longer I who live, but Christ lives in me; and the life which I now live in the flesh I live by faith in the Son of God, who loved me and gave Himself for me."

Rather than live by our works or abilities, we can live by His finished work and His abilities. We were designed to live by His superior, heavenly, divine wisdom. His wisdom will force-multiply our wisdom. Just read about the lives of Joseph and Daniel and see the successful end of their stories. In the same way, when we learn to live in the wisdom of God, His favor will elevate us to a position of influence so that we can impact the world and bring heaven to earth.

Now let me answer your question: "How the heck would I do that?" Well, it's easier done than said. By the way, that wasn't a typo. The answer is Matthew 4:4 and Luke 4:4, "Man shall not live by bread alone, but by every word that proceeds from the mouth of God." Jesus also said, "I only say what I hear the Father say. I only do what I see the Father do." Matthew 4:4 is not talking about the written word, but of the spoken rhema word.

How to Live in His Wisdom

Here's how it works for me: During meetings at work, I would often get ideas that I hesitated to share at that moment. But as soon as I had the thought, someone else always brought it up. This happened so often that I began to speak those ideas, speak what I heard the Father say, so that now the Lord gives me divine strategies in everything I do. I've now become accustomed to saying what I hear the Father say and doing what I see the Father do. That's how I walk in His wisdom. Remember, you enter His rest, not by living by your own efforts or abilities, but by effortlessly living in His finished work and by the abilities He has freely given you. In fact, this Saturday morning, that is how I am writing this book. He is dictating and I am writing. President Obama has an electronic teleprompter, while I have a supernatural One! Mine is better than Obama's! I don't have to think my thoughts. I just have to hear His thoughts and act on them. How can you possibly be stressed if you live like that?

Don't think, "This guy must be a really spiritual dude. That's how he is able to walk in this psychic stuff!" First, this is how God designed us to live. Second, I'm just an ordinary dude like you. You are as special to God as Benny Hinn or Joel Osteen or anyone else. You are His child just like anyone else. Jesus said in John 10:27 "My sheep hear my voice." He speaks to you just as you speak to your kids, and over time you will start getting used to hearing His voice. It is the most natural thing in the world, like walking or talking. You don't have to say, "God told me this or God told me that." You and He are one. God

Chapter 10: Effortless Living in His Amazing Grace

isn't speaking separately from you. When He speaks, you speak. You don't need to say, "God told me to do this, that or the other." You do something because He told you to do it. You and He are so much in love. You do everything together, just as you and your spouse do everything together, actually even more so. When you say something, you and God are saying it together. He backs up everything you say.

You have His wisdom, not just in hearing His voice and speaking it, but also in divine strategies in whatever you do. Most of us have been taught dualistic thinking—that spiritual things are separate from our other activities. We think spiritual activities include going to church on Sunday, morning devotions like prayer and Bible reading and listening to spiritual songs and messages on the drive to or from work. We think the rest of our activities, like what we do at work, taking care of our kids, cooking, cleaning, watching movies, going to the park and everything else is non-spiritual. We have separated spiritual activities from what we think are non-spiritual activities because of our dualistic thinking. In essence we do all those spiritual activities so that God may help us in our non-spiritual activities. So after our so-called spiritual activities, we set God aside and do our so-called non-spiritual activities by our own efforts and abilities.

No, God created you uniquely like Him to live every aspect of your life here on earth with Him and His abilities. You don't have a spiritual side and a natural (fleshly) side. God is living your life with you, in you and through you. Now, who is in your every thought, word and action? God, the Almighty, Supernatural Creator of heaven and earth! You are not simply a body with a spirit. You are a spiritual being, created in the image and likeness of God and indwelt by Him! So you are naturally supernatural! Everything you do naturally is supernatural! In Him we live and move and have our being! He is doing everything you do with you, in you and through you!

How else do you pray without ceasing? Prayer isn't a one-way communication. It is you speaking to God and Him speaking to you. Actually, prayer is more than just communication. It is talking, walking and doing. Prayer is a lifestyle. All through the day, He shows you when and who to talk to. He tells you what you should speak. He shows you what you should do. He shows you how to raise your kids. He teaches you grace-based parenting. When you go shopping, He guides you to the best deals. You and He pick the color of your shirt together. You live in union with God! You live with His wisdom. God is interested in everything you do.

Hakuna Matata

We're looking at how to walk in our inheritance. So far, we have discussed healing and wisdom. Now let's look at joy.

Is it possible to be perpetually happy? How is it that some people wear permanent smiles? I must admit that by nature I'm a serious person. On the other hand my wife Selvi, and my kids Priya and Prakash, are lighthearted and fun loving. While my kids were growing up, I was always the party-pooper, self-disciplined and law-based. From childhood, Selvi was fun loving and made people laugh. From 1990 to 2000, I was a computer programmer, so all day long I was always in deep thought at work, which made me even more serious. People used to tell me that I never smiled. From 1994-1998 we lived in Tampa, Florida. Rodney Howard Browne, who was well known for his laughter revival, moved to Tampa in 1994, and I used to attend all his meetings. He sometimes had forty-day meetings, where I would be filled with joy, and I loved it! But then, after it eventually 'wore off' I returned to being my serious self. At that point I began to search for the answer to this question: How can I be joyful always?

Chapter 10: Effortless Living in His Amazing Grace

Over the years, the Lord has taken me on a journey and showed me several things that were stealing my joy. Even before 1994 I was aware of some of them, like worry and unforgiveness.

I recently asked my wife, Selvi whether I was a happy person. Her response was that I am always a happy person. Actually, I haven't always been a happy person, but these truths have set me so free that Selvi has forgotten what a serious person I used to be.

Some readers may not have seen the 'Lion King' movie. So please bear with me while I set the stage for this section.

'Lion King' is an animated Disney movie that tells the story of Simba, a young lion who was to succeed his father, Mufasa, as king. However, after Simba's uncle Scar kills Mufasa, Simba is deceived into thinking he's responsible and flees into exile in shame and despair. During that time, he lives with two wastrels, Timon, a meerkat and Pumbaa, a warthog. They sing a song called 'Hakuna Matata', that means, "Don't worry, be happy."

One of the keys to happiness is to be worry-free.

Even before I came to a saving knowledge of Jesus Christ, I wasn't a worrier. I love the passages in Matthew 7 and Luke 12 where Jesus describes the futility of worrying. Even back in the eighties I preached sermons on forgiveness and living a worry-free life. I know some folks who are champion worriers. However, the truth is that living carefree is one of the secrets to living a happy life. Now, that doesn't mean living an irresponsible life. As I described earlier in this chapter, we each spend the inheritance that God has given us, but we needn't be burdened down with the cares and worries of life. We can live effortlessly by His wonderful grace. That is one of the keys to happiness: Don't worry, be happy! A couple of years ago we went on a cruise to the Caribbean. One of the countries we visited was Jamaica, where the people are pretty good at this.

Forgiveness

Forgiveness is another key to happiness. While Jesus was on earth He used The Lord's Prayer[4] as a model, teaching His disciples to forgive others and receive His forgiveness. It is easier to forgive others when we understand and believe that God has forgiven us. Though forgiveness has always been easy for me, even before I was saved, the Lord has propelled me to a new level of freedom and joy when I learned the truth that Jesus has forgiven me of all my sins, past, present and future. Joseph Prince's books have the complete teaching with Scriptures on this topic. Let me share just a few of the high points of this teaching. When you forgive others, you will be free. What a simple principle. Jesus prayed on the cross for those who were crucifying Him, saying, "Father, forgive them, for they know not what they do." Jesus is a world-class example of forgiveness and our role model in that respect. So was Stephen. When people were stoning him to death he made this statement in Acts 7:60: "Lord, do not charge them with this sin." The moment I grasped the revelation that Jesus has forgiven me of my past, present and future sins, I immediately decided that I would do the same for others. Jesus taught us to pray in Matthew 6, "Forgive us our sins as we forgive those who sin against us." Do you see the automation in this process? This is a divine principle much like the principle of sowing and reaping, and giving and receiving. I started with my wife. And though it hasn't been easy I'm getting better with practice. Forgiveness becomes a habit. As you keep on looking into the mirror to see that you are a forgiver in the image of Jesus, forgiveness will become easier.

Judgment and Anger

Chapter 10: Effortless Living in His Amazing Grace

This goes hand-in-hand with other divine principles, including: 'don't judge' and 'don't be angry'[5]. If you live in an Eastern culture, these two principles are hard to put into practice. Though I've been in the U.S. since 1990 I was raised in an Eastern culture where everyone judges and advises everyone else who is younger or in a lower position than they are, economically or at work, and give them free, unsolicited advice. When I came to the West, I was amazed at the absence of judgment and criticism and the freedom that comes with it.

I'm not saying that no one in the West judges or gives advice, but there is much less of it in the West. Most people here are far more independent and tend to mind their own business. In the East, everyone else's business is your business. Well, I've had a steep learning curve, but after twenty-four years, I'm finally learning to adapt with this fabulous aspect of the western culture, and as a result, I'm experiencing a much greater degree of freedom. Now, there are many areas in which the West can learn from the East. But this is not a book on cultural differences. So I won't get into that now.

One of the visions of the kingdom of God is a society where no one takes offense. If you don't judge, don't get angry and choose to forgive everyone of everything, regardless of what they do, it's difficult to be offended. This may sound impossible to some of you, but once again heaven is the standard and Jesus is our model. Jesus lived this as us and changed us to be like Him. We just need to walk in who we are. Practice makes perfect. As you keep on looking into the mirror to see that you are, loving and joyful in the image of Jesus, you will not judge or be angry. It's all about your identity. Walking in your identity brings incredible freedom. And greater freedom brings a far greater level of joy! God has entered His rest and doesn't judge you or get angry with you; He has forgiven you of everything! You can enter that rest, too. That's exactly what He wants for you! We pray for God's will for our lives. We pray "not my will, but yours" and "make me more like you." To forgive and not judge or be angry is God's will for your life! We are already like Him. We just need to act like it!

What is Your Destiny?

Have you ever wondered what your destiny is? God created you as a free person to write your own destiny. For the longest time, I thought God had some pre-determined plan for our lives. God created you to be all that He wanted you to be—holy, righteous and perfect. He then filled you with His fullness. He is now in you and with you. You can choose to live your life with Him or without Him. You can write your destiny together with God or without Him. Your destiny is in your hands!

Guilt, Shame, Insecurity and Fear

Now let's look at more joy-robbers—guilt, shame, insecurity and fear. My traditional erroneous beliefs kept me in almost perpetual guilt and shame. This stifled my personality and hindered me from relaxing in my identity as a child of God. I was in great bondage and didn't even know it. I was shackled by guilt, shame, insecurity and fear most of the time. Now I am free and happy as can be! Hakuna Matata!

Let me describe the cycle of guilt, shame, insecurity and fear. Scenario 1 is the description of my life 30 years back. Scenario 2 is my experience after I received a basic revelation of His forgiveness.

Scenario 1: Before 1985

I woke up every morning, knelt by my bed and begged His forgiveness for all the bad things I could think of from the previous day. My prayer was one of introspection, repentance (mourning, wailing and feeling really bad about myself), confession and promises to God, saying, "Lord, I'll never do that again." Now, most of the things I felt guilty about were insignificant things like something I said to someone, negative thoughts that I had about someone and so on. After a few minutes of this, I started picturing the cross, Jesus hanging on the cross with the crown of thorns on His head and his nail-pierced hands. Then I felt sorry for Him and even worse about myself. In time, I mustered enough faith to believe He had forgiven me, and I felt a level of peace come upon me. Then the thanksgiving phase came. I thanked God for forgiving me of each of those sins. Then I basked in His forgiveness, feeling clean, as if I was forgiven.

But it wasn't long before I said or did something that I felt was displeasing to God. This caused me to be consumed by guilt. Shame followed. Insecurity and fear were a natural result because I felt God was angry with me and that I would be disciplined, punished or face some negative penalty like sickness or a loss of one kind or another. Remorse followed, and then repentance, confession and promises. This cycle went on all day long, and I was miserable—a complete emotional wreck by the afternoon. This resulted in poor self-esteem, a poor self-worth and a very bad self-image. Does this ring a bell with anyone? I know that this concept is totally foreign to those who have recently come to a saving knowledge of Jesus and walked directly into the wonderful grace teachings. But I was in utter bondage. How could anyone be happy with that mindset?

Well, in the mid-eighties, I got a better revelation about forgiveness. I was taught that we should keep short accounts with God and that if I confessed my sins, and believed that He forgave me, His blood would immediately cleanse me. So my life changed to the following scenario.

Scenario 2a

I would wake up every morning and go through my introspection. Not realizing that I was already like Him, I would pray, "Make me more like you, Jesus." I thought I was becoming holier by the day. At that time, I thought that I was about 20% holy—hence the introspection. But because I kept short accounts with God and thought I had more faith I would recall all the things from the previous day that I needed to improve. I then repented, but without the mourning and wailing of the past. At that point I believed that He was true to His Word and would instantly forgive me. As you can imagine, that cycle took much less time than the previous cycle. I then prayed in tongues for a while, read the Word for a while until I felt that I was filled with His presence. I took my shower, had my breakfast, and was off to work. But then, I would have a negative thought about someone and felt instant guilt. But because I followed the short-account paradigm, I soon asked God for forgiveness, believed that He forgave me and then thanked Him and went on my merry way. But I felt that somehow such events drained me of the presence and power of God. After attending several meetings at work, and interacting with a lot of folks I had gone through that cycle several times. And though I still suffered from guilt, shame, insecurity and fear, it wasn't as traumatic as before. I also had my self-esteem, self-worth and self-image issues. By evening, I felt I was completely drained of His presence and power.

Scenario 2b

Now, I will describe Scenario 2b with a slight twist. Once in a while, I encountered a situation where someone did something really bad to me. So I got angry and expressed myself accordingly. Since I was already out of fellowship with God because of my sin, I figured that I might as well have a field day while I was at it before I repented again. So I would yell at my wife and kick the dog before I asked for and received His forgiveness for all the sins together.

In Scenarios 2a and 2b, there was still a fear of retribution from an angry God who would judge me for all I did wrong. So for most of the day, I lived in a mixture of guilt, shame, insecurity and fear.

Trying to Become Who You Already Are

For many years I was living in bondage under that paradigm. I was on a constant treadmill of works, striving for purity and perfection, but I was never good enough. This left me with poor self-confidence that reflected in every area of my life. People who were bold and self-confident easily intimidated me.

The funny thing was, with the Word of Faith teaching, I believed I was righteous. I would quote 2 Corinthians 5:21 and tell everyone that their righteousness was their hotline to heaven and the channel of God's blessings. But because of the dual-nature mindset, I still had to subdue my flesh by the Spirit and stay prayed up to maintain right relationship with God to the best of my ability. I was always striving to be the person I thought God wanted me to be. Little did I realize that I was trying to become what I already was, like the swan in the ugly duckling story, the captive eagle before it realized its identity, and like Simba, before he realized that he was king of the jungle.

Now tell me, where is happiness in this model? I wasn't free. All day long, I was tormented by guilt, shame, insecurity and fear! It didn't help my self-esteem, self-worth or self-image.

The Grace Model

Okay, now let's look at the grace model.

Now I wake every morning as happy as a lark, with a song on my lips and a skip in my step. I no longer have a trace of guilt, shame, insecurity or fear. I am filled with His joy and peace. In His presence is fullness of joy and at His right hand are pleasures ever more. I am filled with the fullness of God. I wake up knowing that I am holy. I am righteous. I am perfect, in the image and likeness of God. I don't have to pray for an hour to obtain His favor or anointing. I am His beloved son in whom He is already well pleased. I don't have to read the Word to be pleasing to Him. He's already pleased with me. I'm accepted in the beloved. But when I think of His goodness I just want to be with Him, not just in the morning, but every moment of every day. My lifestyle is a lifestyle of prayer, both in word and deed. I'm one with Him. Now I'm drunk in His presence going to work because I'm an open heaven. Angels of God are ascending and descending over me all day long. I am an in-between creature, in heaven and earth at the same time, seated at the right hand of God. When He ascended, I ascended. I only speak what I hear the Father speak, and I only do what I see the Father do. I am a hotline to heaven. I am a two-way broadband high-speed dedicated line to heaven. Anyone can say anything to me, and I can't get offended. Anger isn't an issue anymore. I now see the better side of everyone. I am a forgiving machine. I forgive everyone before they can say or do anything to me. I am an automatic forgiver. Love overflows from my heart to everyone around me. Everyone is wonderful, whether they are believers or not. The love of God pours through me to everyone I meet. My joy is contagious, and I bring life to every meeting I attend. I receive His divine strategies all throughout the day, and I'm always full of energy. I encourage everyone every chance I get. I ooze self-confidence, and nothing and no one intimidates me. Life is good!

    This is stress-free, effortless living in His abundant grace! You are doing everything, not by your own efforts or abilities, but by His amazing grace. You are a two-way conduit to heaven. You reach into heaven all day long and bring heaven to earth—

impacting the world for Jesus!

Some of you are thinking, "What has this guy been smokin?" Folks, this is how Jesus lived. You are made in His image. You are just like Jesus. Just look into the mirror and keep on looking, and before long you'll see who you are. It doesn't have to take ten years for you to become holy, righteous and perfect. The moment you get this revelation, your holiness, righteousness and perfection will be manifest. As soon as this revelation hits you and you see yourself for who you really are, your true beauty will emerge. The ugly duckling will cease to exist, and the beautiful swan will strut, with her beautiful head held high. You are unstoppable! You are a firebrand for Jesus!

Every day can be like Friday! You can be happy and free! Life will be good for you! Life will be a breeze! You can live in perma-glory all the days of your life!

Notes

Notes

Chapter 1: The Primary Purpose of Creation

1. Rabe, Andre, Adventures in Christ. Andre Rabe Publishing. 2011. Used by Permission
2. 1 John 4:8
3. Miller, Mike, Relax Series. http://www.fathershousefc.com/messages.html?start=42#.U5PFaJGzDwI. Fort Collins: Father's House Ministries.. Used by Permission
4. Toit, Francois Du. Divine Embrace. Hermanus, South Africa: Author, 2012. Used by Permission
5. Toit, Francois Du. Mirror Bible. S.l.: Mirror Word, 2012. Used by Permission
6. Rabe, Andre. Hearhim.net
7. Hebrews 1:3
8. Ephesians 1:4; Psalms 139:16; Jeremiah 1:5

Chapter 2: The Incarnation

1. Toit, Francois Du. Mirror Bible. S.l.: Mirror Word, 2012. Used by Permission
2. Rabe, Andre. Hearhim.net. Used by Permission
3. Toit, Francois Du. Divine Embrace. Hermanus, South Africa: Author, 2012. Used by Permission
4. Crowder, John. Mystical Union. Santa Cruz, CA: Sons of Thunder Ministries & Publications, 2010. Used by Permission.
5. Kruger, C. Baxter. Jesus and the Undoing of Adam. Jackson, MS: Perichoresis, 2003.

6. Kruger, C. Baxter. The Great Dance: The Christian Vision Revisited. Vancouver: Regent College Pub., 2005
7. Genesis 22:13
8. Galatians 2:20 (Darby Version), Philippians 3:9, Mark 11:22
9. Barth, Karl. Dogmatics in Outline. New York: Harper & Brothers, 1959
10. Barth, Karl. The Humanity of God. Richmond: John Knox, 1960
11. Torrance, T. F., & Walker, Robert. Incarnation: The Person and Life of Christ.. IVP Academic. 2008
12. Ephesians 4:13
13. Dunn, Benjamin. The Happy Gospel!: Effortless Union with a Happy God. Shippensburg, PA: Destiny Image, 2011.
14. 2 Corinthians 5:19
15. 2 Corinthians 5:21
16. 2 Corinthians 5:14
17. Young, William P. The Shack: A Novel. Newbury Park, CA: Windblown Media, 2007
18. Genesis 1
19. 2 Corinthians 5
20. Colossians 1:27, 1 Corinthians 6:17
21. Ephesians 1:20

Chapter 3: God is Full of Grace

1. Ephesians 1:3; 2 Peter 2:3
2. Ephesians 3:20
3. John 3:16
4. Hebrews 4:15

5. Toit, Francois Du. Mirror Bible. S.l.: Mirror Word, 2012. Used by Permission

Chapter 4: Grace and Sin

1. 2 Corinthians 5:14
2. John 8:11
3. Crowder, John. Mystical Union. Santa Cruz, CA: Sons of Thunder Ministries & Publications, 2010. Used by Permission.
4. Toit, Francois Du. Mirror Bible. S.l.: Mirror Word, 2012. Used by Permission
5. Prince, Joseph. Destined to Reign: The Secret to Effortless Success, Wholeness and Victorious Living. Tulsa, OK: Harrison House, 2007

Chapter 5: Grace, not Works

1. 1 Corinthians 11:29
2. Galatians 2:20
3. Romans 11:19
4. Isaiah 53:5
5. 1 Timothy 1:7
6. Romans 5:5
7. Philippians 4:19
8. Philippians 4:13
9. 1 Peter 1:8
10. Philippians 4:7
11. Toit, Francois Du. Divine Embrace. Hermanus, South Africa: Author, 2012. Used by Permission

12. Munroe, Myles. *Understanding Your Place in God's Kingdom: Your Original Purpose for Existence.* Shippensburg, PA: Destiny Image, 2011. Used by Permission.
13. John 7:38
14. Colossians 1:27
15. Galatians 2:20 Darby; Philippians 3:9; Mark 11:22
16. Genesis 3:14; Hebrews 13:8
17. Ephesians 4:13
18. Song of Solomon 4:7
19. John 3:16
20. Isaiah 54:9
21. Ephesians 2:6
22. Colossians 1:27; Galatians 2:20
23. Matthew 28:20
24. Romans 8:31
25. Toit, Francois Du. *Mirror Bible.* S.l.: Mirror Word, 2012. Used by Permission
26. Pena, Ryan http://www.spiritandlifesa.com.
27. Miller, Mike. *Welcome Home—Opening the Door to the Nature of God.* Fort Collins: Father's House Ministries, 2013

Chapter 6: Are we only 1/3 Saved?

1. Romans 12:2
2. 1 Corinthians 6:19
3. Romans 6:13
4. Crowder, John. Mystical Union. Santa Cruz, CA: Sons of Thunder Ministries & Publications, 2010. Used by Permission.
5. Genesis 17:1
6. Toit, Francois Du. Mirror Bible. S.l.: Mirror Word, 2012. Used by Permission
7. Pena, Ryan http://www.spiritandlifesa.com
8. Prince, Joseph. Destined to Reign: The Secret to Effortless Success, Wholeness and Victorious Living. Tulsa, OK: Harrison House, 2007.
9. Miller, Mike. http://www.fathershousefc.com/messages.html#.U5Txy5Gz Dwl. Fort Collins: Father's House Ministries. Used by Permission

Chapter 7: The Inclusion Question

1. Colossians 1:11
2. 2 Corinthians 5:14-21
3. Ephesians 4:13
4. Ephesians 1:4, Jeremiah 1:5 and Psalms 139:14,15
5. 1 Corinthians 6:17, Galatians 2:20, Colossians 1:27, Colossians 2:9, 10
6. Galatians 2:20 Darby, Philippians 3:9, Mark 11:22
7. Galatians 2:20

Chapter 8: Living Under an Open Heaven

1. Genesis 28:16
2. Genesis 1:26
3. Ephesians 1:6

Chapter 9: The Kingdom of God

1. Munroe, Myles. Understanding Your Place in God's Kingdom: Your Original Purpose for Existence. Shippensburg, PA: Destiny Image, 2011. Used by Permission.
2. Pena, Ryan http://www.spiritandlifesa.com
3. Crowder, John. Seven Spirits Burning- Santa Cruz, CA: Sons of Thunder Ministries & Publications, 2010. Used by Permission
4. Colossians 1:27
5. Colossians 2:9,10
6. Hebrews 1:3
7. Exodus 7:1
8. Daniel 7:27
9. Isaiah 55:11
10. Toit, Francois Du. Divine Embrace. Hermanus, South Africa: Author, 2012.

Chapter 10: Effortless Living in His Amazing Grace

Notes

1. Munroe, Myles. *Understanding Your Place in God's Kingdom: Your Original Purpose for Existence.* Shippensburg, PA: Destiny Image, 2011. Used by Permission.
2. Prince, Joseph. *Health and Wholeness through the Holy Communion.* Singapore: 22 Media, 2009.
3. Hebrews 1:3
4. Matthew 6

Made in the USA
Columbia, SC
11 September 2024